LIBRARY
COLLEGE OF THE REDWOODS
EUREKA, CALIFORNIA 95501

D1790687

```
OVERSIZE
GV
881      Walsh, Loren
W34
1977       Inside softball
```

DATE DUE

52721

LIBRARY
COLLEGE OF THE REDWOODS
EUREKA, CALIFORNIA 95501

inside softball

inside softball

loren walsh

HENRY REGNERY COMPANY · CHICAGO

Library of Congress Cataloging in Publication Data

Walsh, Loren.
   Inside softball.

   Includes index.
   SUMMARY: Techniques of the game of softball accompanied by a brief history.
   1. Softball.   [1. Softball]   I. Title.
GV881.W34   796.357'8   76-42446
ISBN 0-8092-8017-5
ISBN 0-8092-7887-1 pbk.

Copyright © 1977 by Loren Walsh
All rights reserved
Published by Henry Regnery Company
180 North Michigan Avenue, Chicago, Illinois 60601
Manufactured in the United States of America
Library of Congress Catalog Card Number: 76-42446
International Standard Book Number: 0-8092-8017-5 (cloth)
                                                0-8092-7887-1 (paper)

Published simultaneously in Canada by
Beaverbooks
953 Dillingham Road
Pickering, Ontario, L1W 1Z7
Canada

contents

	Introduction: A Brief History	vii
1	Playing Field and Equipment	1
2	The Rookie Pitcher	7
3	The Fielding Pitcher	17
4	Pitching Style and "Stuff"	25
5	The Complete Pitcher	37
6	The Catcher	45
7	Playing the Infield (Part I)	55
8	Playing the Infield (Part II)	65
9	Playing the Outfield	79
10	Hitting and Running	87
11	Offensive Strategy	103
	Appendix: League and Tournament Scheduling	107
	Index	115

THE FIRST MEN'S World Tournament was held in Mexico City. The United States, represented by the Aurora, Illinois, Sealmasters, won the championship with a 10-0 record.

introduction: a brief history

Credit for originating the game of softball has been given to George Hancock, of Chicago, Illinois. According to historians, the first game was played using a boxing glove for the ball. As the story goes, a group of young men were waiting at the Farragut Boat Club for telegraph returns of the Yale-Harvard football game. The year was 1887; it was Thanksgiving day.

One of the young men threw an old boxing glove at a buddy. He in turn hit it with something resembling a broomstick. Supposedly, Hancock then grabbed the glove and, using the laces, tied it into a sphere and shouted, "Let's play ball."

After the pickup game in the old gymnasium ended, Hancock went home and made a crude ball bigger than a regular baseball. He compiled a list of rules for playing the game in a small area. The new game was called Indoor Baseball.

During the winter of 1887 the game became popular in Chicago, and several teams were organized in various parts of the city. In fact, it caught on so well the game was eventually played outdoors in the spring and summer of 1888. At that time the name was changed to Indoor-Outdoor. Within a few years the game spread to other areas of the country. In 1889 Hancock published his first set of standard rules, which were sold in all parts of the United States.[1]

As the game continued its rapid growth, a great variety of rules evolved. It is estimated that at least a dozen different size balls were being used, and bats varied greatly in length, weight, and design.

In 1933, a committee, the Amateur Softball Association (ASA) met for the purpose of establishing a standard set of rules. Eventually this rules committee became known as the International Joint Rules Committee on Softball (IJRC). At the present time softball is played worldwide with one set of rules.

More than 26 million adults and youngsters of both sexes play softball in the United States annually. In fact, softball is the largest team participation sport in the country today. Although there are still three sizes of balls used, 12-inch, 14-inch, and 16-inch, the 12-inch is by far the most popular. Without question the 12-inch fast-pitch game became the most popular in the early years primarily due to the remarkable exhibitions put on by the underhand pitchers.

NATIONAL TOURNAMENT FAST PITCH

In 1933 the first fast-pitch national tournament for both men and women was held in Chicago, Illinois. From 1933 through 1939 the nationals remained in Chicago. From 1940 through 1943 the tournament was played in Detroit, Michigan. Cleveland, Ohio became the host city for the tournament from 1944 through 1947. In 1948, and for that year only, Portland, Oregon was selected as the site of the national fast-pitch tournament.

The year 1949 marked the first time that the men's and women's fast-pitch tournaments were held in different locations. Other than 1951, when both the men's and women's tournaments were held in Detroit, Michigan, the practice of holding the tournaments in different locations has continued throughout the latter years.

Throughout the first 10 years of the national men's tournament, no team had won the championship two years in a row. Then in 1943 and 1944 Hammer Field of Fresno, California came out victors both years. The year 1945 marked the entry of the Zollner Pistons of Fort Wayne, Indiana into the winners' circle of national champions. In 1946 and 1947 the Zollners repeated and became the first and only team ever to win three national championships in a row.

Although the Zollner Pistons remained in the softball picture until 1954, the team elected not to enter the national tournament. Most softball experts believe that the Pistons would have been capable of winning the national tournament at least five more times had they wished to compete. Although some will disagree, most softball oldtimers believe the Zollner Pistons was the greatest team ever assembled.

The Zollner organization was one of the moving forces that helped establish the great National Fastball League. This league operated from 1946 to 1950 and then temporarily disbanded operations during the Korean War.

The league was divided into two divisions, with Briggs Beautyware (Detroit, Michigan), the 720 Athletic Club (Columbus, Ohio), Dow Chemical (Midland, Michigan), Dayfus Roofers (Windsor, Ontario), Zollner Pistons (Fort Wayne, Indiana), and the Joe Louis Punchers (Flint, Michigan) comprising the Eastern Division.

Metal Parts Corporation (Racine, Wisconsin), Pilots (Waukegan, Illinois), Merchants (Aurora, Illinois), Rockets (Rock Island, Illinois), Milwaukee, Wisconsin, Shafer Pen (Iowa City, Iowa), and State Farm Insurance (Bloomington, Illinois) made up the Western Division.

Probably the finest fast-pitch league ever organized, the National Fastball League ceased operations in 1954. Dow Chemical, Briggs Beautyware, Zollner Pistons, and the Aurora Sealmasters (Aurora Merchants' replacement) were all national ASA champions at one time or another. The final game for the league playoff championship was played in Aurora, Illinois between Briggs Beautyware, of Detroit, and the Aurora, Illinois Sealmasters, on September 14, 1954. Detroit won the final game 3-2, in eight innings. Detroit's John Spring, later elected to the ASA hall of fame, defeated Aurora's Chick Walsh, author of *Inside Softball*.

In 1950, the Clearwater, Florida Bombers won the National Championship at Austin, Texas. From 1950 to 1973, three teams, the Clearwater Bombers, Raybestos Cardinals, of Stratford, Connecticut and the Aurora Sealmasters dominated the National Championships. During that period the Bombers claimed the title 10 times. Raybestos Cardinals were national champions five times and the Aurora Sealmasters copped the title four times. Only Dow Chemical (1951), Burch Tool, of Detroit (1964), and Welty Way, of Cedar Rapids, Iowa (1971) managed to unseat these three softball dynasties.

National Championship winners in women's fast-pitch also reflect a three-team dominance. From 1942 until 1973 the Jax Maids, of New Orleans, Louisiana; Lionettes, of Orange, California; and Raybestos Brakettes, of Stratford, Connecticut have combined to win 25 titles.

WOMEN'S WORLD TOURNAMENT

In 1965, the first worldwide Women's Championship was held in Melbourne, Australia. Five countries competed, with the U.S. highly favored to win. Surprisingly, the host Australian team defeated the U.S. entry 1-0 in the final championship game.

The second women's world tournament was hosted by Japan, in 1970. Again the U.S. was heavily favored to walk away with the crown. This time ten countries were represented. When the smoke had cleared, the host Japanese team ended with a 9-1 record, including a 1-0 victory over the U.S., to win the World Championship. A record crowd of more than 30,000 witnessed the final game between the U.S. and the host Japanese team.

Stratford, Connecticut was the site for the 1974 Women's World Championship. This was the first time the entrants were divided into two divisions, with a total of 15 teams competing. The winner was decided by a round robin, plus a play-off series. For the first time, the U.S. team was a world champion, with nine wins and no defeats.

MEN'S WORLD TOURNAMENT

The first world championship for men was held at Mexico City, in 1966. The U.S., represented by the Aurora, Illinois Sealmasters, dominated play and came out on top with a record of 10 wins and no losses. A U.S. world tournament representative is determined by the winner of the previous year's National Championship.

In 1968, at Oklahoma City, the U.S.—again represented by the Sealmasters—were crowned world champions and posted a 10-1 record. The only loss was a 2-0 upset by Puerto Rico. After the 1968 tournament, the International Softball Federation decided to hold the tournament every four years instead of the previous two-year cycle. Manila was the site of the 1972 World Championships, in which 10 teams competed. Canada emerged as world champions and the U.S., represented by Welty Way, of Cedar Rapids, Iowa finished a close second.

FAST-PITCH DECLINE

Fast-pitch reached its greatest level of popularity in the middle forties. As previously mentioned, one major factor for its rapid growth was the novelty of watching spectacular underhand pitching performances. However, as the pitchers became more and more advanced, the number of strikeouts per game soared. Obviously, this had the effect of reducing the action and, likewise, spectator interest. In addition, wealthy sponsors began recruiting larger and better pitching staffs. This was necessary to cope with the 90- to 120-game schedules.

By enlarging pitching staffs and enticing outstanding players to join their team, these organizations created an elite group of softball teams. And this produced a situation that few softball enthusiasts anticipated. It drastically reduced the number of pitchers available for smaller sponsors. Without good pitchers the smaller sponsors, which were the foundation of fast pitch, gradually began disbanding their teams. The long-range effect was a lack of interest in the game universally and fewer youngsters were exposed to the game. As a result, the young pitchers were not being developed.

EMERGENCE OF SLOW PITCH

These previously mentioned factors opened the door for a new and exciting game, 12-inch slow pitch. At first the game was thought to be for older players, retired from fast pitch. As the game developed and gained stature, however, it proved to be anything but an old men's or old ladies' game. Its growth even exceeded that of the early fast pitch, and presently more than 80 percent of softball participants are playing slow pitch of some type.

The first national slow-pitch tournament for men was held in Cincinnati, Ohio, in 1953. Cincinnati was also the first site of the Women's National Tournament, held in 1962.

Slow pitch offers the participant a lot of action, as hits and runs are plentiful. The game also has a unique built-in feature. It offers an opportunity for the fierce competitor to participate in very tough leagues. But it also provides the average person who wishes an outlet for recreation a chance to play on his local neighborhood team. People of both sexes and all ages, all over the world, have found slow pitch one of the most enjoyable team sports available.

FAST PITCH RETURNING

During the last several years, fast pitch has started to regain its former popularity. Although pitching is still a very dominant factor, hitters are catching up and the average strikeouts per game has gradually dropped.

Through youth programs sponsored by various community groups and with the assistance of concerned individuals, interest in fast pitch is on the rise once again. For example, Harvey Sterkel, one of the greatest pitchers of all times, has devoted a great deal of his time to helping young pitchers. Results of his efforts are evident, as both of his sons have become outstanding hurlers.

Sterkel, a member of the Aurora Sealmasters and holder of several national records, is a strong advocate of youth softball programs. He contends that the average youngster is anxious to participate in fast pitch and all he needs is a little encouragement and proper instruction.

Girls' fast pitch has recently become a regular part of the athletic program in many of our high schools and colleges. In 1976, a women's professional league was established and has gained a considerable following.

Many of the smaller towns that had discontinued softball programs have now established new leagues for both men and women. At present the ASA currently provides National Tournament competition in the 13-15 and 16-18 age groups for both fast and slow pitch.

This book, *Inside Softball,* is directed to the young softball enthusiast wishing to learn and the adult player who is seeking ideas for improvement. Because fast-pitch techniques are such a key factor in the game, there has been greater emphasis placed on this aspect of the sport. Although the material presented in the following chapters concentrates heavily on fast pitch, most of it is equally applicable to the slow-pitch game.

---

1. *The Softball Story,* by Morris A. Bealle, published by Columbia Publishing Co., 1957.

NATIONAL SOFTBALL CHAMPIONS FAST PITCH (MEN)

Year	Champions
1933	At Chicago, Illinois — J. J. Giths, Chicago, Ill.
1934	At Chicago, Illinois — Ke Nash-A's, Kenosha, Wisconsin
1935	At Chicago, Illinois — Crimson Coaches, Toledo, Ohio
1936	At Chicago, Illinois — Kodak Park, Rochester, New York
1937	At Chicago, Illinois — Briggs Mfg. Co., Detroit, Michigan
1938	At Chicago, Illinois — Pohlers, Cincinnati, Ohio
1939	At Chicago, Illinois — Carr's, Covington, Kentucky
1940	At Detroit, Michigan — Kodak Park, Rochester, New York
1941	At Detroit Michigan — Bendix Brakes, South Bend, Indiana
1942	At Detroit, Michigan — Deep Rock Oilers, Tulsa, Oklahoma
1943	At Detroit, Michigan — Hammer Field, Fresno, California
1944	At Cleveland, Ohio — Hammer Field, Fresno, California
1945	At Cleveland, Ohio — Zollner's Pistons, Ft. Wayne, Indiana
1946	At Cleveland, Ohio — Zollner's Pistons, Ft. Wayne, Indiana
1947	At Cleveland, Ohio — Zollner's Pistons, Ft. Wayne, Indiana
1948	At Portland, Oregon — Briggs Beautyware, Detroit, Michigan
1949	At Little Rock, Arkansas — Tip-Top Clothiers, Toronto, Canada
1950	At Austin, Texas — Clearwater Bombers, Clearwater, Florida
1951	At Detroit, Michigan — Dow Chemical Co., Midland, Michigan
1952	At Stratford, Connecticut — Briggs Beautyware, Detroit, Michigan
1953	At Miami, Florida — Briggs Beautyware, Detroit, Michigan
1954	At Minneapolis, Minn. — Clearwater Bombers, Clearwater, Fla.
1955	At Clearwater, Florida — Raybestos, Stratford, Connecticut
1956	At Sacramento, Calif. — Clearwater Bombers, Clearwater, Fla.
1957	At Clearwater, Fla. — Clearwater Bombers, Clearwater, Fla.
1958	At Minneapolis, Minn. — Raybestos, Stratford, Connecticut
1959	At Clearwater, Florida — Sealmasters, Aurora, Illinois
1960	At Long Island, N. Y. — Clearwater Bombers, Clearwater, Fla.
1961	At Clearwater, Florida — Sealmasters, Aurora, Illinois
1962	At Stratford, Conn. — Clearwater Bombers, Clearwater, Fla.
1963	At Clearwater, Fla. — Clearwater Bombers, Clearwater, Fla.
1964	At Sunnyvale, California — Burch Tool, Detroit, Michigan
1965	At Clearwater, Florida — Sealmasters, Aurora, Illinois
1966	At Indianapolis, Ind. — Clearwater Bombers, Clearwater, Fla.
1967	At Springfield, Mo. — Sealmasters, Aurora, Illinois
1968	At Clearwater, Fla. — Clearwater Bombers, Clearwater, Fla.
1969	At Springfield, Missouri — Raybestos Cardinals, Stratford, Conn.
1970	At Clearwater, Fla. — Raybestos Cardinals, Stratford, Conn.
1971	At Springfield, Mo. — Welty Way, Cedar Rapids, Iowa
1972	At Dallas, Texas — Raybestos Cardinals, Stratford, Conn.
1973	At Seattle, Wash. — Clearwater Bombers, Clearwater, Fla.
1974	At Clearwater, Fla. — Guanella Bros., Santa Rosa, Calif.
1975	At Hayward, Calif. — Rising Sun Motel, Reading, Pa.

NATIONAL SOFTBALL CHAMPIONS FAST PITCH (WOMEN)

Year	Champions
1933	At Chicago, Illinois — Great Northerns, Chicago, Illinois
1934	At Chicago, Illinois — Hart Motors, Chicago, Illinois
1935	At Chicago, Illinois — Bloomer Girls, Cleveland, Ohio
1936	At Chicago, Illinois — National Mfg. Co., Cleveland, Ohio
1937	At Chicago, Illinois — National Mfg. Co., Cleveland, Ohio
1938	At Chicago, Illinois — J. J. Kreig's, Alameda, California
1939	At Chicago, Illinois — J. J. Kreig's, Alameda, California
1940	At Detroit, Michigan — Arizona Ramblers, Phoeniz, Arizona
1941	At Detroit, Michigan — Higgins "Midgets," Tulsa, Oklahoma
1942	At Detroit, Michigan — Jax Maids, New Orleans, Louisiana
1943	At Detroit, Michigan — Jax Maids, New Orleans, Louisiana
1944	At Cleveland, Ohio — Lind & Pomeroy, Portland, Oregon
1945	At Cleveland, Ohio — Jax Maids, New Orleans, Louisiana
1946	At Cleveland, Ohio — Jax Maids, New Orleans, Louisiana
1947	At Cleveland, Ohio — Jax Maids, New Orleans, Louisiana
1948	At Portland, Oregon — Arizona Ramblers, Phoenix, Arizona
1949	At Portland, Oregon — Arizona Ramblers, Phoenix, Arizona
1950	At San Antonio, Texas — Orange Lionettes, Orange, California
1951	At Detroit, Michigan — Orange Lionettes, Orange, California
1952	At Toronto, Canada — Orange Lionettes, Orange, California
1953	At Toronto, Canada — Betsy Ross Rockets, Fresno, California
1954	At Orange, California — Leach Motor Rockets, Fresno, California
1955	At Portland, Oregon — Orange Lionettes, Orange, California
1956	At Clearwater, Florida — Orange Lionettes, Orange, California
1957	At Bueno Park, California — Betsy Ross Rockets, Fresno, California
1958	At Stratford, Conn. — Raybestos Brakettes, Stratford, Conn.
1959	At Stratford, Conn. — Raybestos Brakettes, Stratford, Conn.
1960	At Stratford, Conn. — Raybestos Brakettes, Stratford, Conn.
1961	At Portland, Oregon — Gold Sox, Whittier, California
1962	At Stratford, Conn. — Orange Lionettes, Orange, California
1963	At Stratford, Conn. — Raybestos Brakettes, Stratford, Conn.
1964	At Orlando, Florida — Erv Lind Florists, Portland, Oregon
1965	At Stratford, Conn. — Orange Lionettes, Orange, California
1966	At Orlando, Florida — Raybestos Brakettes, Stratford, Conn.
1967	At Stratford, Conn. — Raybestos Brakettes, Stratford, Conn.
1968	At Stratford, Conn. — Raybestos Brakettes, Stratford, Conn.
1969	At Tucson, Arizona — Orange Lionettes, Orange, California
1970	At Stratford, Conn. — Orange Lionettes, Orange, California
1971	At Orlando, Florida — Raybestos Brakettes, Stratford, Conn.
1972	At Tucson, Arizona — Raybestos Brakettes, Stratford, Conn.
1973	At Stratford, Conn. — Raybestos Brakettes, Stratford, Conn.
1974	At Orlando, Fla. — Raybestos Brakettes, Stratford, Conn.
1975	At Salt Lake City, Utah — Raybestos Brakettes, Stratford, Conn.

NATIONAL SLOW PITCH CHAMPIONS (OPEN DIVISION)

Year	Champions
1953	At Cincinnati, Ohio — Shields Contractors, Newport, Ky.
1954	At Louisville, Ky. — Waldeck's Tav., Cincinnati, Ohio
1955	At Pittsburgh, Pa. — Lang's Pet Shop, Covington, Ky.
1956	At Cleveland, Ohio — Gatliff Auto Sales, Newport, Ky.
1957	At Toledo, Ohio — Gatliff Auto Sales, Newport, Ky.
1958	At Cleveland, Ohio — East Side Sports, Detroit, Mich.
1959	At Cleveland, Ohio — Yorkshire Rest., Newport, Ky.
1960	At Toledo, Ohio — Hamilton Tailoring, Cincinnati, Ohio
1961	At Louisville, Ky. — Hamilton Tailoring, Cincinnati, Ohio
1962	At Cleveland, Ohio — Skip Hogan A. C., Pittsburgh, Pa.
1963	At Jones Beach, N. Y. — Gatliff Auto Sales, Newport, Ky.
1964	At Springfield, Ohio — Skip A. C., Pittsburgh, Pa.
1965	At Maumee, Ohio — Skip A. C., Pittsburgh, Pa.
1966	At Parma, Ohio — Michael's Lounge, Detroit, Mich.
1967	At Parma, Ohio — Jim's Sport Shop, Pittsburgh, Pa.
1968	At Jones Beach, N. Y. — County Sports, Levittown, N. Y.
1969	At Parma, Ohio — Copper Hearth, Milwaukee, Wis.
1970	At Southgate, Mich. — Little Caesar's, Southgate, Mich.
1971	At Parma, Ohio — Pile Drivers, Virginia Beach, Va.
1972	At Jacksonville, Fla. — Jiffy Club, Louisville, Ky.
1973	At Cleveland, Ohio — Howard Furniture, Denver, N. C.
1974	At York, Pa. — Howard Furniture, Denver, N. C.
1975	At Cleveland, Ohio — Pyramid Cafe, Lakewood, Ohio

NATIONAL SLOW PITCH CHAMPIONS (WOMEN'S DIVISION)

Year	Champions
1962	At Cincinnati, Ohio — Dana Gardens, Cincinnati, Ohio
1963	At Cincinnati, Ohio — Dana Gardens, Cincinnati, Ohio
1964	At Omaha, Nebraska — Dana Gardens, Cincinnati, Ohio
1965	At Omaha, Nebraska — Art's Aces, Omaha, Nebraska
1966	At Burlington, N. C. — Dana Gardens, Cincinnati, Ohio
1967	At Sheboygan, Wisc. — Ridge Maintenance, Cleveland, Ohio
1968	At Cincinnati, Ohio — Escue Pontiac, Cincinnati, Ohio
1969	At Chattanooga, Tennessee — Converse Dots, Hialeah, Fla.
1970	At Parma, Ohio — Rutenschroer Floral, Cincinnati, Ohio
1971	At Satellite Beach, Florida — Gators, Ft. Lauderdale, Fla.
1972	At York, Pa. — Riverside Ford, Cincinnati, Ohio
1973	At Chattanooga, Tennessee — Sweeney Chevrolet, Cincinnati, Ohio
1974	At Elk Grove, Cal. — N. Miami Dots, Miami, Fla.
1975	At Jacksonville, Fla. — N. Miami Dots, Miami, Fla.

TYPICAL SOFTBALL EQUIPMENT.

chapter 1
PLAYING FIELD AND EQUIPMENT

A softball playing field is defined as that part of the grounds that lies between the foul lines and 25 feet outside the foul lines. This area must be clear and unobstructed within a radius from home plate as described below:

- 225 feet (male and female fast pitch)
- 250 feet (female slow pitch)
- 275 feet (male slow pitch)

A playing field that has its unobstructed area enclosed by a fence avoids many confusing ground rules. When a playing field is not limited by a fence, ground rules covering obstacles must be agreed upon by opposing teams or leagues.

The diamond area of the playing field must always be carefully measured and chalked using the official distances specified. To lay out a diamond area, always start with home plate. If laying out a field for the first time, be sure to put home plate where the sun will always be behind the catcher.

After home plate is located, drive a stake at the corner nearest the catcher. Fasten a cord to the stake and tie or mark four places along the cord. Measuring from the stake, tie or mark the cord at a distance of 46 feet, 60 feet, 84 feet 10¼ inches, and at 120 feet.

Take the cord toward the center of the diamond and hold taut without stretching. Place the 46-foot marker of the cord down when the cord is lined up, cutting home plate in two equal parts. At the 46-foot marker, drive a stake. This stake will be the location of the middle of the front edge of the pitcher's plate. The pitching distance (back corner of home plate to front edge of pitcher's plate) of 46 feet is correct for all softball diamonds unless it is to be used for female fast pitch. In that case, the pitching distance should be set at 40 feet.

After the stake for the pitcher's plate has been placed, continue in the same line with the cord until reaching the 84-foot, 10¼-

FIELD AND EQUIPMENT

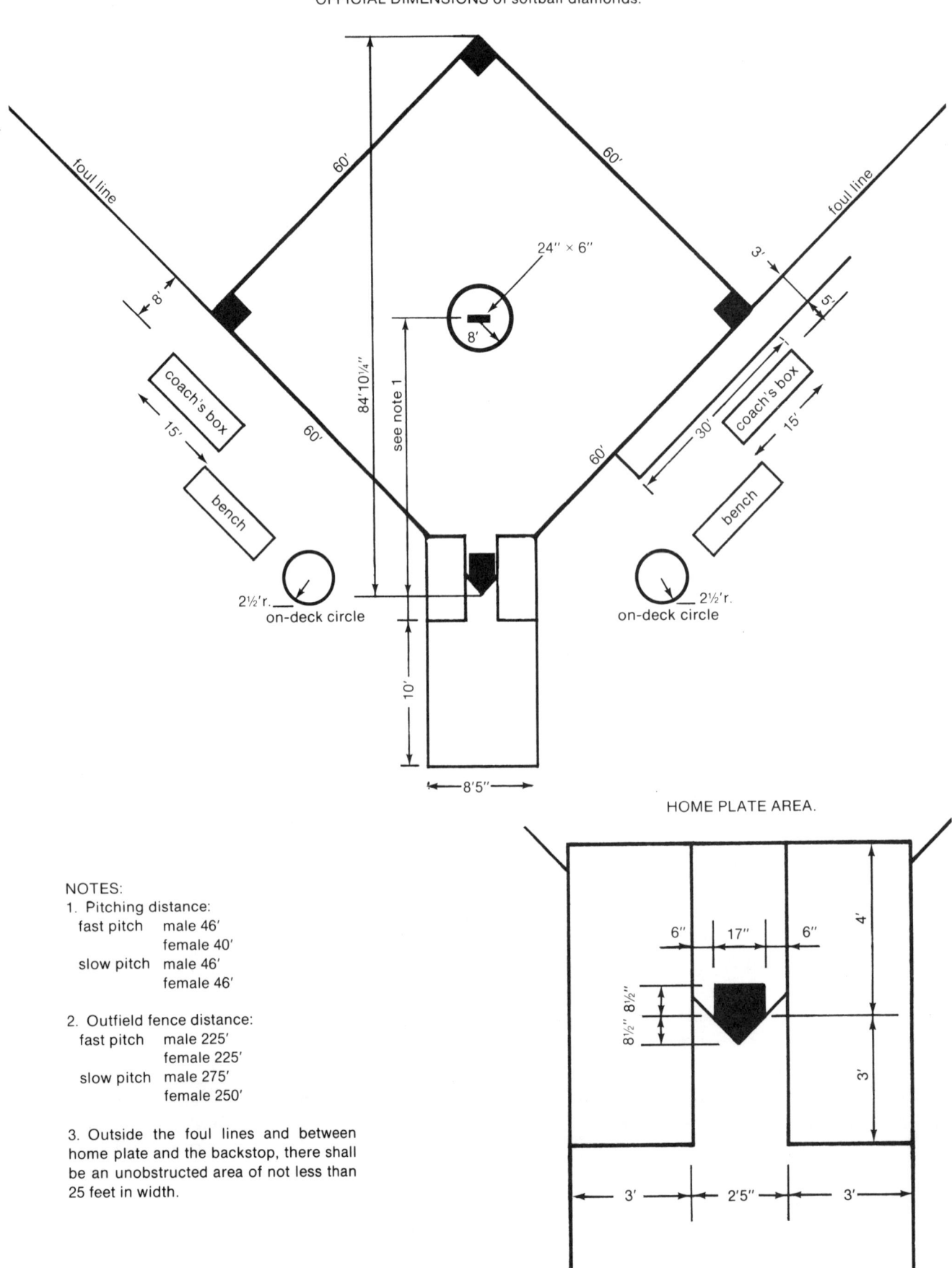

OFFICIAL DIMENSIONS of softball diamonds.

HOME PLATE AREA.

NOTES:
1. Pitching distance:
   - fast pitch   male 46'
   -                 female 40'
   - slow pitch   male 46'
   -                 female 46'

2. Outfield fence distance:
   - fast pitch   male 225'
   -                 female 225'
   - slow pitch   male 275'
   -                 female 250'

3. Outside the foul lines and between home plate and the backstop, there shall be an unobstructed area of not less than 25 feet in width.

inch mark. Holding the cord taut without stretching, drive a stake at this marker. The center of second base will be set at this point.

Find the 120-foot mark on the cord and secure this to the second base stake. Now find the 60-foot marker on the cord and walk away from the line of home plate and second base until the cord is again taut. Drive a stake at the 60-foot marker. Do the same thing on the opposite side. These two stakes will now determine the outside corner of first base and third base.

It is advisable to check the diamond layout. This is easily done by taking the cord from the home plate stake and placing it on the first-base stake. Secure the 120-foot mark to the third-base stake. When the cord is held taut at that point, the 60-foot marker should check out at home plate and in the opposite direction at second base. It is a good idea to recheck all distances with a steel tape.

TEAM EQUIPMENT

Softball bats will generally be furnished by the team. Team bats will usually be of different lengths, weights, shapes, and materials. With a number of choices, the player can usually find the bat that feels comfortable for his use. The more serious player may have his own personal bats that he has carefully selected from the large number available in sporting goods stores.

Whatever bat is used it must be an official softball bat which has been clearly marked "Official Softball" by the manufacturer. An official bat will be round and may be made from metal, wood (one piece), plastic, bamboo, or laminated wood. It may not exceed 38 ounces in weight.

Metal bats must have their exposed surfaces free of burrs and any rough or sharp edges. Exposed rivets, pins, or any form of exterior fastener that would present a hazard is unacceptable on the metal bat. Also, metal bats are not permitted to have a wooden handle.

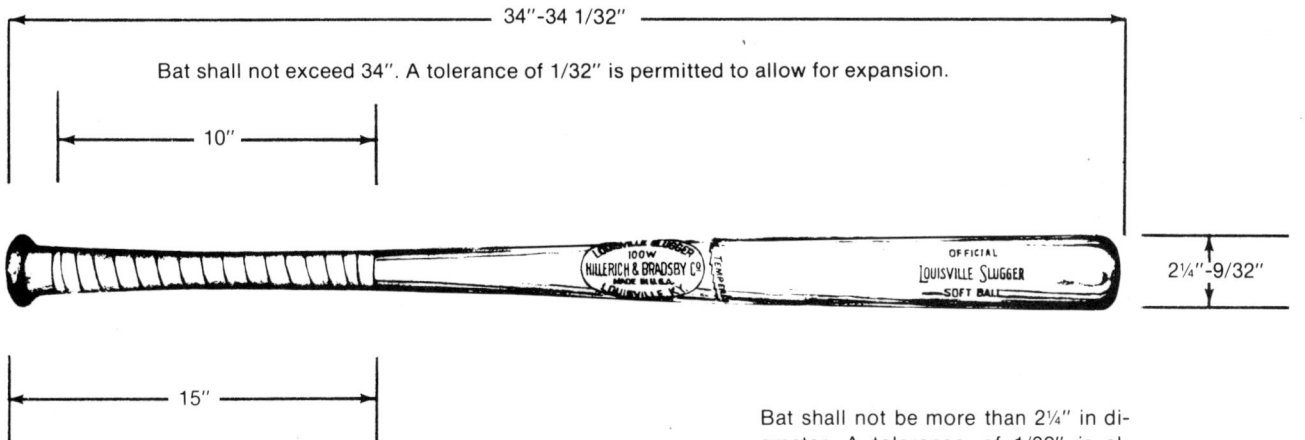

OFFICIAL BAT SPECIFICATIONS.

Safety grip shall be no less than 10" long. It shall not extend more than 15" from small end of bat.

Bat shall not be more than 2¼" in diameter. A tolerance of 1/32" is allowed for expansion.

Wooden bats may be made from either one piece of hardwood or from a block of laminated wood. When laminated wood is used, the individual pieces of wood must be bonded together in such a way that the grain direction of all the pieces is parallel with the length of the bat.

Plastic and bamboo bats have no special requirements other than those that apply to all official softball bats in general.

The official bat may have a size no greater than 34 inches long or 2 9/32 inches in diameter. It must have a safety grip of cork, tape, or composition material that is no less than 10 inches long. A safety grip must not extend more than 15 inches from the small end of the bat. If the bat is not made of one piece construction with the barrel end closed, there must be a rubber or vinyl plastic insert firmly secured at the large end of the bat.

When the physical structure of a legal bat has been changed, it is called an altered bat by the rulebook. Some examples of what would be considered an altered bat are:

- Replacing the handle of a metal bat with a wooden handle or other type handle
- Inserting material inside the bat
- Adding a foreign substance, such as paint, to a bat

Replacing one safety grip with another legal safety grip is not considered altering the bat.

When a batter appears in the batter's box with, or is discovered using, an altered bat he will be called out.

Softball

New or "game" balls are furnished by the home team for use during game play. Usually those balls that have already been used for a game are kept for practice and warm-up drills.

The official softball is a smooth-seamed concealed stitch or flat surfaced ball, between $11\frac{7}{8}$ and $12\frac{1}{8}$ inches in circumference (distance around the outside), and shall weigh between $6\frac{1}{4}$ ounces and 7 ounces. It must have a center made of either No. 1 quality long fibre kapok or a mixture of cork and rubber, hand or machine wound, with a fine quality twisted yarn and covered with latex or rubber cement. Other materials may be used for the center of the ball if they are approved by the International Joint Rules Committee on Softball. Outside covering of the ball shall be the finest quality No. 1 chrome tanned horsehide or cowhide, cemented to the ball by application of cement to the under side of the cover and sewed with waxed thread of cotton or linen. Synthetic material may also be used to cover the ball.

Catcher's Equipment

Protective equipment for the catcher is normally furnished by the team. A mask, chest protector, helmet, and shin guards are usually made available to the catcher for his use. A mask must be worn in fast pitch and is suggested for slow pitch.

Uniform

All players on a team must wear uniforms identical in color, trim, and style. Ball caps are considered a part of this uniform for male players. Undershirts exposed to view and worn by more than one member of the team must be of the same color, and the color shall be uniform and solid. No player may wear a uniform shirt or exposed undershirt that has ragged, frayed, or slit sleeves.

To reduce the possibility of injury, no player may wear exposed jewelry during a game. Examples of exposed jewelry items that are common and must be removed are wristwatches, bracelets, and neck chains. Rules permit protective helmets to be a part of the uniform for catchers, batters, and baserunners.

PERSONAL PLAYER EQUIPMENT

A player is expected to furnish his own shoes and glove or mitt. Shoes may have soles which are either smooth or have soft or hard rubber cleats. Metal sole and heel plates may be used if the spikes on the plates do not extend more than three-quarter inch from the shoe's sole or heel. Shoes with rounded metal spikes are illegal.

A ball player's glove or mitt may be compared to the infantryman's rifle. His performance depends upon it. A glove or mitt becomes as much a part of the player's arm as his hand when he takes the field. Not only does the player keep his glove or mitt with him constantly, but he keeps it clean and in good condition.

A glove may be worn by any member of the team; however, only the catcher and the first baseman are allowed to wear a mitt. No glove or mitt may have top lacing, webbing, or other device between the body and thumb more than four inches in length. The pitcher's glove must be of one color other than white or gray. Multicolored gloves may be worn by all other players as long as they do not have white or gray circles that give the appearance of a ball.

PRESENTATION POSITION must be held for at least one second.

chapter 2
THE ROOKIE PITCHER

Certain countries always produce good teams and top athletes in a given sport. Canada, for example, has outstanding hockey players. For many years, Australia developed the finest tennis players in the world. In recent years, the U.S. has returned from the Olympic games with the lion's share of gold medals in swimming.

One major reason for these successes is outstanding coaches and well-organized instructional programs. In almost every case, this training began when the participants were very young. I don't completely agree with the idea that one cannot teach an old dog new tricks, but it is certainly more difficult.

As I mentioned earlier, one reason for the slow growth of fast pitch in recent years has been the lack of top-notch pitchers. Many knowledgeable softball people feel this situation was created by the absence of youth softball programs. If the former popularity of fast pitch is to return, it must come through new instructional programs that help encourage younger players to play fast-pitch softball. Suggestions for teaching the young pitcher are presented in this chapter.

AVERAGE GROUPS

From an average group of youngsters, one can expect a great difference in talent. Some will not only have natural coordination, but they also will have mastered some advanced skills. On the other hand, a few will be poorly coordinated and will not have developed even the basic skills for throwing and catching.

The problems faced in teaching athletic skills are very much the same as those of teaching in the classroom. A teacher must spend more time with the slow pupil, while trying to keep the interest of the faster learner.

IT SHOULD BE FUN

Most practice sessions turn into two or

three hours of boring drills. Too many coaches lose sight of the purpose of practice. A practice is a learning experience, and learning must be interesting to the student as well as the teacher.

When faced with a variety of talent, methods can be used to prevent boring practice sessions. For example, youngsters who need more work on fundamentals may be invited to practice earlier than the more advanced group. With a little initiative, this can be done without hurting the slower youngsters' feelings.

Other ideas—such as asking the pitchers, catchers, and infielders to come at different times—will prevent situations where some are standing around for long periods. Breaking up batting practice into two or three periods also will liven up practice. There is nothing more boring than standing in the outfield for an hour and then getting only three or four minutes of batting practice. Coaches can do many other things to create and hold the interest of the young player.

Over the years, coaches and managers develop their own individual teaching techniques. A method that is successful for one may be completely wrong for another. Nevertheless, all good coaches and classroom teachers seem to have some type of natural talent for evaluating ability.

When the classroom teacher wishes to be sure of his opinions, he gives some type of test to the student. Unfortunately, coaches and managers seldom use test and measurement programs even though they are available. An advantage of prepared testing methods is the ability of these tests to determine characteristics and player capabilities that may be overlooked by the busy coach. Another benefit is the fact that these tests can pick up changes. When the tests are given periodically, certain areas of learning improvement will be noted clearly.

Regardless of how the coach measures the players' potential, those players having natural talent usually will stand out during the first few practices. In fact, it's common for the coach to find that his best pitching prospects are also his best infielders and outfielders. In addition to natural talent, eagerness and willingness to learn are important considerations for choosing the most likely pitching prospect.

THE FIRST STEP

Rather than trying to throw hard and put "stuff" on the ball, early practice workouts should be spent on very simple fundamentals. One of the first fundamentals to be learned is how to take the proper stance on the mound.

A pitcher must place both feet firmly on the ground and be in contact with the pitching rubber, but neither foot can be at the side of the rubber. Before pitching the ball, he must come to a complete stop and face the batter. Both shoulders should be in line with first and third base, and the ball must be held in both hands in front of the body. This position must be held at least one second, but not more than 20 seconds, before taking one hand off the ball to start the delivery. These time requirements were made for special reasons. The time of the one second pause was put into the rule book to prevent the "quick pitch" (pitching the ball before the batter is ready). The 20-second time limit prevents stalling.

You are not considered to be in a pitching position unless the catcher is in position to receive the ball, so it is very important to be sure the catcher is ready. Also, the pitcher is not in the proper pitching position on or near the rubber without having the ball. This rule discourages the use of the "hidden ball trick" and prevents a pitcher from unfairly forcing a runner back to a base.

THE ROOKIE PITCHER 9

LEGAL

ILLEGAL

LEGAL

ILLEGAL

LEGAL

ILLEGAL

BOTH FEET must be firmly on the ground and in contact with, but not off the side of, the rubber.

REGULATION PITCH

A regulation pitch begins as soon as one hand is taken off the ball or the pitcher starts any type of motion that is part of the windup. In the actual act of pitching the ball, the pitcher is allowed only one stride, or step, and this must be forward and toward the batter. The rear foot (pivot foot) must stay on the pitching rubber until the ball is released.

By strictly following the above regulations, a pitcher will not develop bad habits. For example, some pitchers drift into the habit of sliding the rear foot, or in some instances the front foot, off the mound to get extra momentum before pitching. Once this fault has become a regular part of the windup rhythm, it is very difficult to correct.

There have been instances where pitchers have pitched for years with an illegal motion before it was discovered. Usually, this error is detected in a very important game. An umpire will normally issue a warning, but since the habit has been developed over a long period, the error will be repeated. The penalty for this is termed an illegal pitch and a "ball" is immediately called by the umpire. All runners then automatically advance one base.

Legal Delivery

A legal delivery is one in which the ball is pitched to a batter with an underhand mo-

PRESENTATION POSITION—hold one second.

BACKSWING and forward stride.

tion. The release of the ball and the follow-through of the hand and wrist must be forward, past the straight line of the body. As the arm passes this straight line of the body, the hand must be below the hip, and the wrist no farther from the body than the elbow. In other words, a sidearm or a "submarine" baseball motion is not permitted.

Keep in mind that the rule for a legal delivery does not forbid the wrist and hand from being outside the elbow just before passing the straight line of the body. In fact, this extension of the wrist and hand beyond the elbow is the way that much of the "stuff," or rotation, is put on the ball. Although this explanation of rotation of the ball may be slightly difficult for the very young player to understand, it should be noted here in the event he observes and questions these characteristics of pitching used by some of the advanced teenage or adult pitchers.

The Windup

Any windup may be used providing it meets the following regulations: No motion to pitch can be made without immediately delivering the ball. In other words, the pitcher may not fake a motion to pitch, hesitate, stop, or reverse his forward motion.

A pitcher may not use a rocker motion. For example, after holding the ball in both hands in the pitching position, he removes one hand from the ball, makes a backward

THE UNDERHAND motion with hand below hip.

SMOOTH FOLLOW-THROUGH with front foot pointed straight ahead.

and then forward swing and returns the ball to both hands in front of the body.

No more than one complete revolution of the arm may be made. This applies to the windmill-type motion which will be discussed more thoroughly in a later chapter. It should be noted that the pitcher may drop his arm to the side or the rear just before starting the windmill motion. However, he may not continue to windup after taking the forward step which occurs at the same time the ball is released.

Another regulation that should be brought to the attention of the young pitcher is the rule about warm-up pitches prior to the start of the inning. According to the official rules, at the beginning of each inning or when a pitcher relieves another, no more than one minute may be used. Also, no more than five pitches may be pitched to the catcher or any other teammate. During this period, play is stopped. The penalty for too many warm-up pitches is the awarding of a ball to the batter for each pitch more than five.

Starting Out

For all practical purposes, there are two windups used by present-day pitchers. One is the windmill delivery and the other is the slingshot. Detailed explanations of the two styles will be covered in a later chapter. In brief, the windmill consists of one complete revolution of the arm. The slingshot is a delivery where the pitcher first swings the arm to the rear and then snaps it forward while delivering the pitch.

A third style, the figure eight, is very seldom used anymore. In the early years of softball, it was the most popular as well as a very effective delivery. As time passed and the distance from the pitching rubber was lengthened, the figure eight was discarded in favor of the windmill and slingshot styles.

USE THE PITCHING RUBBER

Almost anyplace, indoors or outdoors, can be used for practicing the pitching delivery. But for best results, throw from an actual

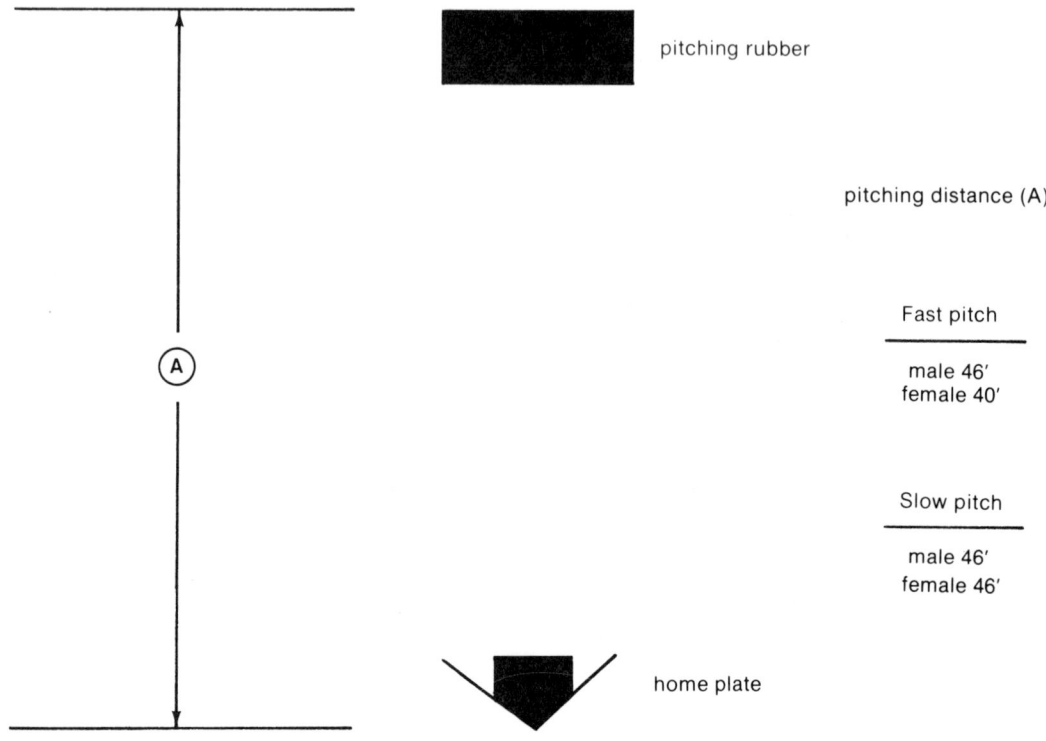

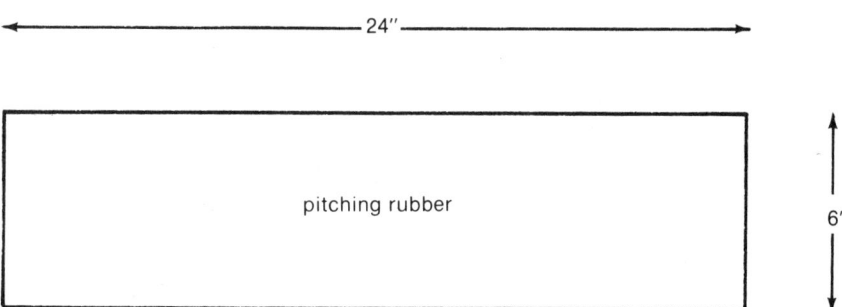

PITCHING RUBBER shall be made of wood or rubber.

pitching rubber whenever possible. Official rules describe the rubber as follows: The pitching plate must be made out of wood or rubber, twenty-four inches long and six inches wide. The top of the pitcher's plate should be level with the ground. Official distance from the front of the pitching rubber to home plate is as follows: Male Fast Pitch (46 ft.); Male Slow Pitch (46 ft.); Female Fast Pitch (40 ft.); Female Slow Pitch (46 ft.).

Whether or not the youngster should start pitching at the official distance of 46 feet is a matter of opinion. Some coaches strongly believe it's best to start at a shorter distance, 40 or 42 feet, for example. The idea in this case centers around the fact that the eight- to ten-year-olds have difficulty controlling the ball well enough to pitch with any accuracy at 46 feet. In addition, they contend pitching the ball at this distance may injure the undeveloped arm.

Of course, the major reason for starting the youngster at 46 feet is that he will not have to adjust to varying distances in future years. However, organized baseball programs for younger players follow the principle of starting the youngster at a closer distance. They do not seem to have any great problem adjusting to the official distance of 60 feet.

Probably the greatest adjustment problem occurs when a well-developed teenager already throwing "stuff" on the ball makes the move from the shorter to standard distance. This opinion is based on past experiences. In 1950, the official distance was moved from 43 to 46 feet. Many pitchers failed to make this adjustment smoothly. Their ability to keep the rise ball in the strike zone became very difficult. As a result, many pitchers gradually disappeared from the fast-pitch scene.

ACTUAL GAME CONDITIONS

During practice, it's just as important to throw to an official home plate as it is to throw from an official pitching rubber. Home plate is a five-sided figure, seventeen inches wide across the edge facing the batter. The sides must be parallel to the inside lines of the batter's box and are eight and one-half inches long. The sides of the point facing the catcher are twelve inches long.

Don't be too concerned about your control and speed at first. It is more important to develop a smooth, comfortable pitching delivery. Too much emphasis on either speed or control may slow your progress. Repeat your delivery over and over until every move feels perfectly natural. As you continue to practice and the delivery becomes comfortable, you'll find that you will be able to throw more strikes with greater speed.

One of the best ways to improve your control is by spending extra hours working with your catcher. During scheduled practice sessions or when you have spare time, have your catcher give you a clear target with his mitt. Take extra time before your windup and stare directly at the position of the catcher's mitt. Even call out the exact location of his glove just before you start your delivery.

Even though it is not possible all the time, the more often you throw with an actual batter in position, the faster your control will progress. When there is no batter available, a chair placed in the batter's box is a good substitute for the batter.

SLOW PITCH

Even though the pitching regulations are not as complicated for slow pitch as fast pitch, careful attention to official rules must not be overlooked. Official rules state that the pitcher must take a position with a foot firmly on the ground and in contact with the pitching rubber. His foot may be in contact with the front, middle, or rear of the rubber, but it cannot be in contact at the side.

Prior to delivery, his arm must come to rest holding the ball in front of his body with the pivot foot in contact with the pitching rubber. He must hold this position at least one second and not more than twenty seconds before starting his delivery. The ball must then be pitched toward home plate on the first forward swing of the pitching arm as it moves past the hip. A pitch starts when you make any motion that is part of the windup. There can be no stop or reversal of this forward motion.

Once your delivery has begun, the pivot foot must stay in contact with the rubber until the ball leaves the hand. There is no particular limit on the position of your free foot except that if a step is taken it must be made at the same time the ball is pitched towards home plate. After you release the ball you may move in any direction you choose.

A legal pitch must be delivered underhand, with the arm passing below the hip. Every pitch must have a detectable arc of at least three feet from the time it leaves the pitcher's hand until it crosses home plate. There is no limit on the height of the pitch, but it must be delivered at moderate speed. In fact, the acceptable speed is left entirely to the judgment of the umpire. If the umpire believes the ball is being pitched too fast, he will warn the pitcher. If the pitcher repeats a fast pitch, the umpire will remove him from the pitching position for the rest of the game.

A pitcher cannot use tape or other substances on the pitching hand or fingers. No foreign substances may be placed on the ball. However, the pitcher can use powdered resin to dry his hands. While pitching, you cannot wear a sweatband, bracelet, or similar items on the wrist or forearm of the pitching arm.

The catcher plays an important role in the pitching routine as he is required to return the ball directly to the pitcher after each pitch, except after a strikeout or put-out made by the catcher. Once the pitcher assumes his pitching position, he has 20 seconds in which to release the next pitch. If he does not comply with this regulation, an additional "ball" is awarded to the batter. Furthermore, the catcher must be in the boundaries of the catcher's box and remain there until each pitch leaves the pitcher's hands.

Under the following conditions "no pitch" will be called: a) A pitcher pitches during the suspension of play, b) A runner is called out for leaving the base too soon, c) The pitcher makes a quick return pitch to the batter, d) If the ball slips from the pitcher's hands during his windup or backswing. In all of these cases, the umpire will signal the ball dead and all action following the pitch will be cancelled.

A legal pitch occurs when the pitcher delivers the ball in accordance with all the previous regulations including the following conditions. At the beginning of each inning or when a pitcher relieves another, no more than one minute of warm-up must be used. In addition, no more than five balls may be pitched to the catcher or any other teammate.

An illegal pitch is called when a pitcher throws to a base while his foot is in contact with the pitcher's plate, or fails in accordance with the ball pitching regulations. In any case of an illegal pitch, the umpire calls the pitch a "ball," and the ball is considered dead. If a batter swings and misses an illegal pitch, it is considered a strike and no penalty is called against the pitcher. There is also no penalty called when the batter swings and hits an illegal pitch.

Just as in fast pitch, the beginning pitcher should also concentrate on learning to field ground balls properly and to back up bases.

ROOKIE PITCHER practices throws to first base under game conditions.

chapter 3
THE FIELDING PITCHER

A majority of softball players will agree that most fast-pitch pitchers are poor fielders. There are two major reasons for this. One, as the pitcher matures, he usually spends less time on fielding and concentrates entirely on the more technical areas of pitching. A second reason, and one that is often overlooked, occurs as a result of the follow-through motion required in fast-pitch softball. Since the follow-through motion of the arm is upward, the pitcher is in an awkward position to field line drives and sharp ground balls, or to charge bunts. However, this is no excuse for the pitcher to shirk his fielding responsibilities.

One way a coach may combat a lack of interest in fielding is to include the pitcher in the infield drills. Hit the ball to him and have him throw to the appropriate base. Furthermore, a pitcher should occasionally play various other positions in the infield during infield practice or in an actual game. In this way, his defensive skills will not slip at an early age.

FIELDING THE BUNT

With the exception of the drag bunt, a bunt is used to advance a runner. Therefore, practically anytime you field a bunt, the throw will be made to an infielder who is moving to cover the proper base. So it is best to practice fielding bunts under the same conditions that would exist in a regular game. Use a runner, or runners, and have the batter actually bunt and run to first base.

Once the bunt is laid down, don't charge it too fast since the ball is often spinning and may change direction. Charge the bunt with feet well apart so you can quickly move in either direction. Gently scoop the ball in your glove hand and quickly place the throwing hand on the ball. It is a good idea to practice this fundamental step many times before looking up and throwing. Most errors are made because the fielder looks up before he actually has a good hold on the ball. By using this very basic exercise even after many years of practice and play-

THE FIELDING PITCHER

CHARGE BUNT with feet well spread.

SCOOP BALL and quickly place throwing hand over it.

ing, your ability to field the bunt will stay sharp.

Since there is usually a runner on base in any potential bunt situation, you must decide quickly where to throw the ball as soon as you field it. This choice must be made in a split second. Therefore, when there is a good possibility of a bunt, size up the situation just before each pitch to the hitter.

If the runner on first is extremely fast, your chance of getting him at second is not good, and you'll probably have to settle for the out at first. This doesn't mean that you should never throw to second. However, it only stands to reason that your throw will be hurried and the percentage of getting the runner is low, while the chance of making an error is high.

Calling the Base

Up to this point, one very important point has not been mentioned. It's the catcher's responsibility to call out to the fielder which base to throw to when an infielder or pitcher fields the bunt. Sometimes it may be impossible to hear the catcher or he may be temporarily shielded by the runner and cannot call out the proper base soon enough. In this case, the pitcher must make a snap decision and throw where he can most likely make the putout.

Runners on First and Second

Let's assume the opposing team has runners on first and second, with nobody out. Once again, determine which base runner is quicker and what you will do if the ball is bunted in your direction. Although a fast runner is more likely to advance safely on a bunt, he is also likely to be farther off base in case the batter pops up on the attempted sacrifice. A bunt that is popped up creates a possible double play, or even a triple play.

A very important consideration to keep in mind with runners on first and second is the danger of a bunted ball getting past the pitcher. Consequently, it is unwise to charge carelessly. Since the first baseman and third baseman will be in close to field the ball, the second baseman will be moving to cover first and the shortstop will be moving to cover third. You can quickly see that if the bunted ball gets past the pitcher, not only will the runners all be safe, but it is entirely possible the runner from second will score.

When first and second are occupied, the pitcher can throw to any base except home for the force out. Nevertheless, it is rare in fast pitch for a pitcher to be able to field a bunt cleanly and get the runner at third.

THE FIELDING PITCHER

CHARGING off mound for bunt.

KEEP GLOVE LOW and get in front of ball.

LEFT-HAND PITCHER often makes complete pivot on throw to first.

Unless the ball is bunted very hard to the pitcher, third base should not be considered a good choice for the force out.

Runners on First and Third

With runners on first and third and none out, the pitcher is facing the most difficult bunt situation in the game. There are many options to be considered. This is one instance where the pitcher, first baseman, or third baseman probably will field the ball since the catcher cannot afford to leave home plate unprotected.

If the runner on third is the tying or winning run in the late innings, you must try to get him rather than throwing to first or second base. When the runner on third is not the winning or tying run, or when the game is in early innings, it is best to cut down the runner at second or at least get the hitter at first for the force-out. Disregard the runner at third. With a man on first and third, the out at home must be a tag, another important reason for attempting to get the force-out at first or second. The options are practically the same with a runner on third only, as they are with a runner on first and third. The exception is that a force at second is not available.

Bases Loaded

Although a team seldom bunts with the bases loaded, a bunt properly placed can be extremely effective in this case. Once more it is essential to review the situation before pitching. Consider the runner's speed and what kind of a bunter the batter is. Obviously, occasions will arise where you may not be familiar with either the batter or the runner. In such a spot as this, when you are not certain what to do, it is just as likely that some of your infielders are also uncertain. Call time out for a quick conference and decide what your best choice may be under the given circumstances.

Going to home for the force out should be your first choice. This is also a good time to consider the possibility of a pop up, and where to go for the possible double play. Your first choice should be third base so that you can cut down the lead run, providing the ball is not hit to a spot that makes it impractical to throw in that direction. If the ball is popped up and it is impossible to double up the runner at third, be very sure that you have a play at another base. A wild throw at this point may allow all three runners to score.

A key tip for all pitchers to remember is

LEARNING ONE OF the pitcher's jobs early: backing up third base.

that some bunts are so well executed that there is no possibility of making a reasonable play at any base. The only choice available is to hold the ball. When to throw and when not to throw are best learned through actual game experience. Remember, it's not a crime to play it cautious in a spot such as this.

BACKING UP THE BASES

Failure of the pitcher to back up bases usually reflects lack of good coaching during the teenage years. Unfortunately, a good many outstanding pitchers who played in the 1940s, 1950s, and 1960s seldom backed up infielders properly.

For the most part, this weakness can be attributed to the era when the game gained its popularity. During these years, the softball pitcher learned his trade on the sandlots and in pick-up games. He rarely had the benefit of learning proper fundamentals of fielding his position.

Many of the more recent pitchers have had the opportunity to play in well organized Little Leagues or similar programs. Although these programs didn't necessarily make him a better throwing pitcher; they did help him to learn how to back up bases. Proper instruction and game experience will teach the pitcher to move almost automatically to back up the proper base following a base hit.

Hit to Right... None On

When a sharp line drive or ground ball is driven into right field and it appears to be going directly at the fielder, the pitcher should move to back up second base. The shortstop will usually take the throw as the second baseman is often out of position, since the line drive or ground ball often requires him to move towards the foul line. The pitcher should make the same move toward second in the event there is a short fly ball to right field.

If the hitter pulls the ball down the right field foul line, or if he hits a very long fly ball, a pitcher must watch carefully to see what develops. At some point in the action he must determine whether a throw will be made to second, third, or home. If he feels the hit will be a triple, he must either back up third base or, if the runner appears to be trying for an inside-the park home run, he must back up the catcher at home plate. Providing the physical dimensions of the field permit, the pitcher should be from 20 to 30 feet behind the fielder covering the base. At this distance he is able to move laterally on a wide throw or stop an extremely high overthrow.

Hit to Left... None On

Every team has its own way of playing defense, but in practically every case when a batter lines a sharp hit into left field, the

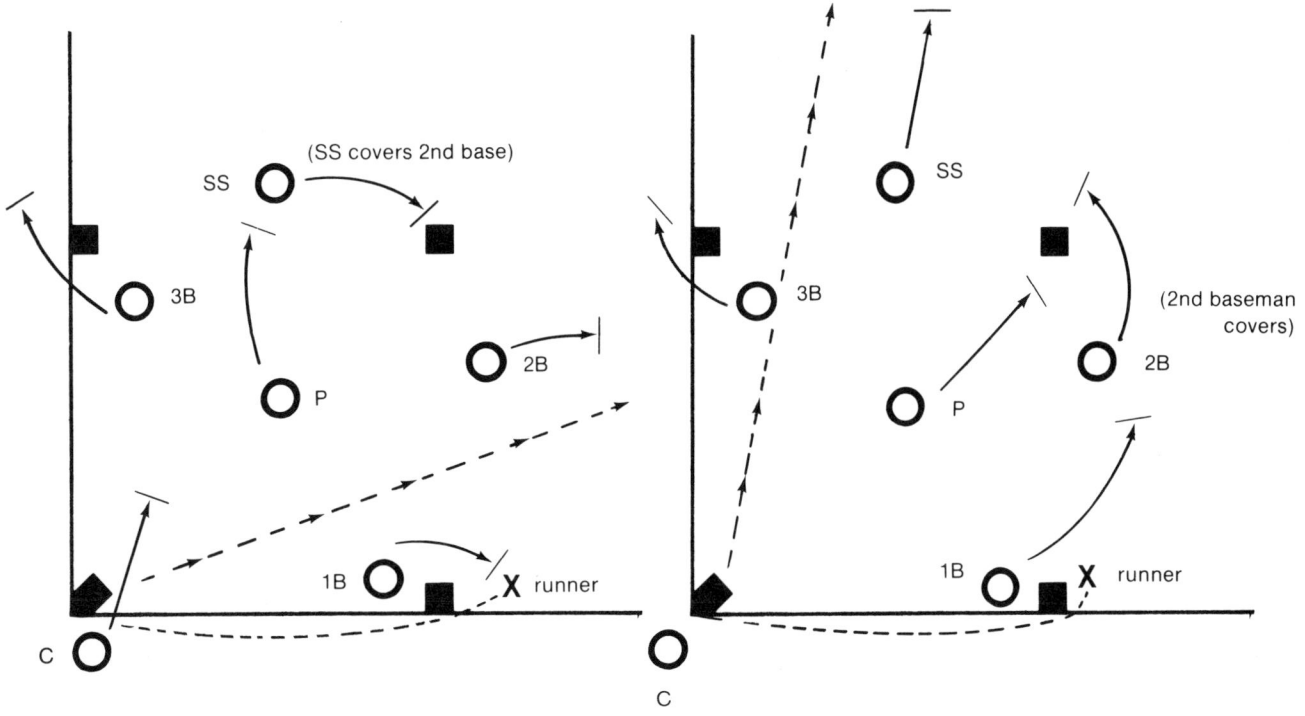

INFIELD MOVEMENT to right field (nobody on). Pitcher backs up second base. Third baseman is deep back-up man.

INFIELD MOVEMENT by single to left field (nobody on). Pitcher backs up second. First baseman is deep back-up man.

first baseman will back up the throw at second base. But if the batter pulls it down the foul line or hits a deep fly ball that may go for extra bases, the pitcher should back up the throw at third base. In this situation, he should be approximately 20 to 30 feet behind the third base and in a line with the left fielder and third base.

Hit to Center... None On

On a sharp single to center field, the pitcher is in excellent position to back up second base. That doesn't mean he should just stand near the pitching rubber after the hit, but rather line himself up with the point from where the center fielder throws and second base.

Either a sharp liner or a long flyball to center that looks like it will go for extra bases is a signal for the pitcher to move toward third to back up the throw from the center fielder. On a short fly ball that causes the center fielder to come in fast to make the catch, the pitcher should be backing up second base. If the center fielder is unable to make the catch or drops the ball, a fast runner will often try for a double.

Runner on First

When first base is occupied, almost any hit to the outfield will advance the runner to second base. Therefore, the pitcher should automatically concentrate on backing up third. However, if first is occupied and the

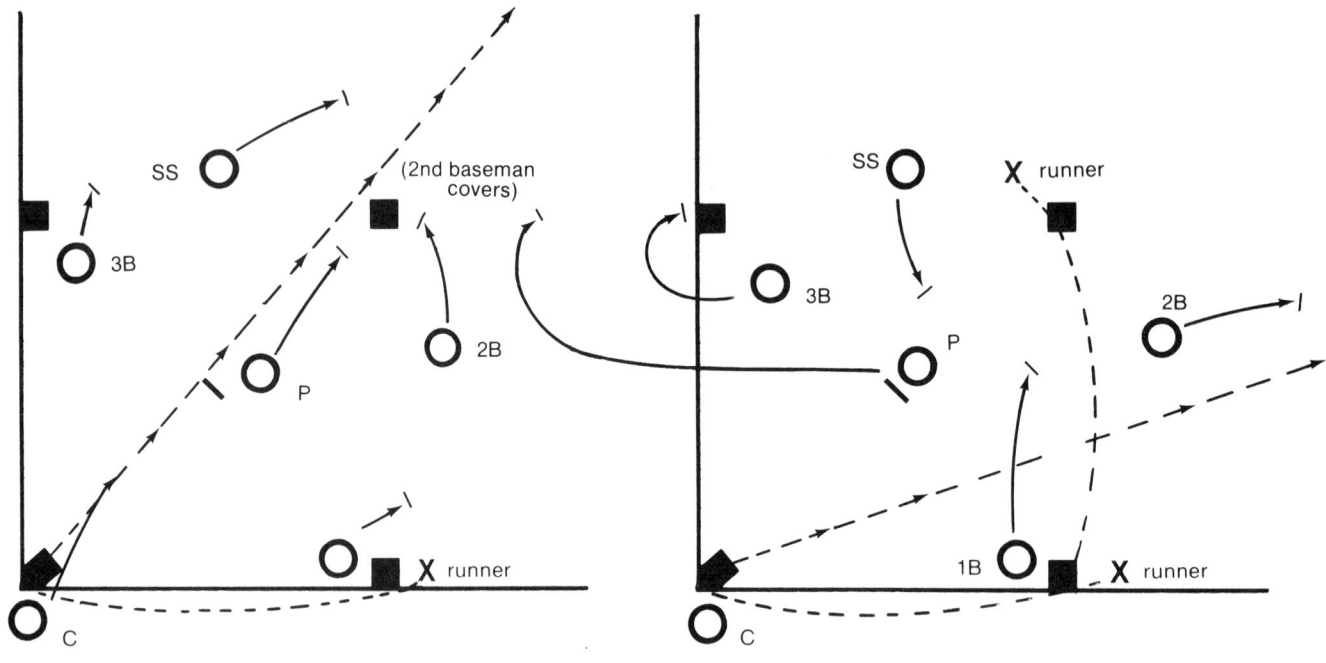

INFIELD MOVEMENT for single to center (nobody on). Pitcher backs up second. Catcher is deep back-up man.

MOVEMENT OF INFIELDERS on single to right (runner on first). Pitcher backs up third base.

batter hits a short fly ball that begins to fall between the infielder and outfielder, a different approach must be considered. First of all, the runner will not be leaving the base too far because he doesn't know whether the ball will be caught or drop in for a base hit.

When the short fly ball is toward the left-field side, the shortstop will be attempting to make the catch along with the left fielder. Consequently, the second baseman will be covering second base and the first baseman will be close to first for a possible double play in the event the ball is caught and the runner has gone too far off the bag. As a result, the pitcher should be backing up second base in the area between first and second. Should the ball be popped up to the right field side, the second baseman will be attempting to make the catch, the shortstop will be covering second, and the pitcher should be backing up second base between second and third.

Runner on Second Only

Approximately 90 percent of the time, a runner on second will score on a hit to the outfield. A good outfielder will usually not make a throw to the plate unless the ball is hit very sharply and directly to him or if the runner represents the winning or tying run. Regardless of where a hit goes, when a runner is on second base, the pitcher must watch carefully how the ball is played in the outfield and where the throw appears to be going.

The best move is to take several steps toward home and turn so you have a good view of the outfield. Should the outfielder throw to the plate and it is obvious a play cannot be made, the pitcher is then in good position to cut off the throw. After you take the cutoff throw, immediately look for the runner in case he is trying for second. Preventing the hitter from advancing to second means it will take an extra base hit rather than a single to score him.

Runner on Third Only

Unless the runner falls, practically any hit to the outfield will score a runner from third. Generally, you can disregard the runner and concentrate on where the batter hit the ball. The one instance when you must concentrate on a runner at third occurs on a short fly ball to the outfield with one or none out. As soon as the pitcher determines that the ball may be caught, he should check to see if the runner is leaving third without tagging. If so, call for the ball to be thrown to third and immediately move to back up third base. On the other hand, when the runner definitely tags up at third, he is in position to score after the catch. Then the pitcher has no choice but to back up the throw at home plate. Even though the runner may not make a break for the plate, the pitcher must be backing up the throw in case the incoming throw gets through the catcher.

Runners on First and Second

Since a hit to the outfield will usually score the runner from second, you as a pitcher must be alert to what happens with the runner who was on first base. However, the score, the inning, and the runner enter into your decision as to what base to back up.

Let's examine the following set of circumstances during a close game in the late innings. Runners with good speed are on first and second, one or none out, and your team is ahead 2 to 1. A batter hits a clean single to the outfield. Remember that the runner from second most likely will score.

The game will be tied, and your outfielder will be trying to keep the first runner from advancing more than one base, so there is a good chance the throw will be to third.

Although we have stressed the point that a runner on second will normally score on a hit to the outfield, there is always the possibility that the ball may be hit so hard that a play at the plate is possible. Therefore, before making a move toward any base, face the outfield, watch to see how the play develops, and be prepared to cut off the throw or to back up third base.

When second and third are occupied or if the bases are loaded, your decision as to what base to back up will depend on the previous basic situations and examples presented. Keep in mind that anytime runners are on base, proper execution of backing up bases after a base hit can be nearly as effective as a strikeout.

A pitcher really should be looked upon as a complete infielder and not just a thrower. With the proper attitude and hard work, he can contribute as much to the defense as any member of the team.

SLOW PITCH

Since the rules for slow pitch do not permit bunting, the pitcher does not have to be concerned with fielding bunts. Because the game is designed to allow the batters to hit the ball on virtually every time at bat, it is necessary for the pitcher to be a very good infielder. A good fielding pitcher in slow pitch has the opportunity to make nearly as many assists as any of the other infielders.

Since there are a great deal of base hits in the game of slow pitch, backing up bases by the pitcher is even more important than in fast pitch. Although the pitching technique for slow pitch is entirely different from fast pitch, the basic fundamentals for backing up bases are the same. Therefore, the previous instructions presented in this chapter for backing up bases in fast pitch can be applied to slow pitch as well.

SLINGSHOT DELIVERY. As arm reaches farthest point of backswing, front leg is fully extended.

chapter 4
PITCHING STYLE AND "STUFF"

From the age of twelve to sixteen, the young pitcher can make great strides toward becoming a good softball pitcher. There have been instances in major softball circles where fifteen- and sixteen-year-olds have pitched in adult softball leagues.

One of the greatest pitchers of all time, Harvey Sterkel, pitched in a regional tournament at the age of sixteen and pitched outstanding ball in national tournament when he was just seventeen. Elmer Rohrs, a member of the Softball Hall of Fame, joined the Zollner Piston team as a teenager.

During these years it is best if the young pitcher settles on the style of delivery that is most comfortable for him. The two major styles are the windmill and the slingshot. Through the years there has been much controversy over which is better. Supporters of each style have provided some very logical reasons why their style is best.

During the mid-1950s, the popular style of the outstanding pitchers was the slingshot. However, since that time there has been a decided trend toward the windmill.

Regardless of what style you settle on, the characteristic of the final swing of the arm is the same for both the slingshot and windmill. Both deliveries require the same action and coordination as the sidearm or overhand motion in baseball. In reality, the underhand softball delivery is a throwing motion and shouldn't be confused with a similar motion used for pitching horseshoes.

Some pitchers have to learn the underhand softball delivery by starting with a regular sidearm baseball motion and then gradually modifying it until they are able to throw a true underhand pitch. Others seem to pick up the underhand delivery with very little effort at a very early age.

SLINGSHOT

The slingshot style is appropriately named since the arm is brought back relatively

26 PITCHING STYLE

START of downward snap.

NOTE cocked wrist for throwing rise ball.

FORWARD foot planted as rise ball is released.

FINAL twist of wrist after release of rise ball.

SMOOTH follow-through of rise ball.

SLINGSHOT DELIVERY (sequence)

slow and then snapped through the arc of delivery similar to an actual slingshot. Becoming comfortable on the pitching rubber will take a little time if you haven't been pitching softball. A right-hander normally places his right foot slightly forward of the left foot. The toe portion of the shoe is positioned in front of the rubber with the heel portion making contact with the rubber. Placement of the left or rear foot differs between pitchers. Usually it is placed approximately four to six inches behind the right foot with the toe portion of the shoe making contact with the rear portion of the rubber. Some pitchers put the left foot directly behind the front foot while others feel comfortable with feet spread apart.

With any type of delivery style you must take the official pitcher's starting position, with both hands in front of the body. At the beginning of the normal slingshot windup, the pitcher's hand is drawn from the glove and moved in a down and backward motion. This motion is continued until the pitching hand is above and behind the head. When you first draw the pitching hand from the glove, lean slightly forward with knees bent and begin your forward stride. When the pitcher's arm is at the furthest point on the backward swing, the front leg should be fully extended. The arm is then snapped forward and the front foot is planted firmly on the ground just prior to the release of the ball.

WINDMILL

Although every pitcher has his own peculiar way of throwing, there are two distinct techniques of the windmill delivery. The regular delivery begins with the pitcher beginning his windup from the official pitching position. As the pitching hand is brought out of the glove, the upper portion of the body is bent slightly forward; the knees are also bent to prepare for the forward stride. The pitching arm is then raised above the head, beginning a circular motion. Although it is difficult to see during the pitching delivery, the arm is slightly bent at the elbow just past the very top of the motion. This fulcrum-type action of the elbow and wrist generates the speed and stuff required in fast pitch. As the arm moves in this complete circular motion, the forward stride continues.

At the same time the ball is released, the forward foot is planted firmly while the rear foot is lifted from the rubber to complete the follow-through. The length of time the rear foot remains in contact with the pitching rubber varies from pitcher to pitcher.

WINDMILL DELIVERY

BODY LEANS slightly forward, knees bent.

BALL REMOVED from glove and start of stride.

ARM RAISED above head.

START circular motion.

AT SAME TIME ball is released, foot is planted.

FOLLOW-THROUGH for curve ball. Throwing arm passes across front of body.

With some, the rear foot is lifted almost simultaneously with the release of the ball. Other pitchers leave the rear foot in contact with the rubber after the release of the ball.

A second type of windmill delivery consists of a combination of the regular windmill and a so-called pump motion. Instead of removing the pitching hand from the glove at the start of the windup, the pitcher lifts both arms upward to his chest, face, or even clear behind his head. As the arms are returned downward, the pitching hand is removed from the glove and dropped down and backward. At this point, the pitcher swings his arm forward and proceeds into the regular windmill delivery.

Many pitchers who use the pump motion feel that it gives them extra momentum, more consistent rhythm and, as a result, more speed. In addition, some of these pump windups are confusing and distracting to the batter.

FOLLOW-THROUGH

A consistent and proper follow-through motion are very important to a pitcher's delivery. There are two major areas to concentrate on in developing good follow-through habits. First, as the ball is released, the arm swing should be a smooth, straight upward motion on each pitch. The final height of the arm on the follow-through will vary with the individual pitcher. Another major area of concern is the placement of the striding foot. On each pitch, the striding foot should be placed in almost the same spot as the ball leaves the pitcher's hand. In order to maintain good balance and be in a good position to field, the foot should be pointed almost directly at home plate. When pitchers develop an awkward follow-through action, their striding foot ends up at a severe angle. They are off balance and have a difficult time fielding a bunt, ground ball, or line drive.

After the release of the ball, bring the rear foot forward and take a slightly crouched position with legs spread and your weight on the balls of your feet. By assuming this position, you can handle any type of batted ball with little lost motion.

An easy way to check foot placement is to rake or sweep the ground at the approximate point where the foot will be. Then observe where the foot is being placed on each type of pitch. A windmill style pitcher often has a tendency to jump off the mound with his rear foot, which leaves the rubber almost simultaneously with the release of the ball. In this case, it is a good idea to check where both feet are being placed.

Jumping off the mound is acceptable by the official rules, providing the ball has been released prior to the jump. However, there has been an increasing trend by windmill pitchers to remove the rear foot prior to the release of the ball. This premature step is referred to as "crow hopping." Some pitchers have been able to get away with this crow hop for many years. But more and more umpires are beginning to call them for illegal pitches. After throwing for many years, it is almost impossible to correct a fault of this nature. Therefore, it is worth the time and effort to learn the proper follow-through when you are beginning to develop your pitching style.

DEVELOPING "STUFF"

There are exceptions to every rule, but in fast pitch, the outstanding pitchers rarely throw a plain fastball. In other words, each pitch has something on it. The most common pitches are the rise ball, drop, and change-up. From each of these three most commonly thrown pitches, other pitches may be developed by slightly varying the grip, rotation, and release.

It is difficult to say at what age you should begin developing an assortment of pitches. Some boys and girls are capable of throwing rise balls and curves in their early teens, while others are not capable of throwing stuff until they are out of high school.

Regardless of when you begin to try to throw stuff, there is one big factor to keep in mind. There is no one best way to grip the ball for throwing a certain pitch. If you ever see an illustration accompanied by instructions that state, "This is the correct way to grip a curve ball," change the word "correct" to "one way." To repeat the previous comment, there is no one correct or best grip for throwing a particular pitch.

Actually the grip is second in importance to the proper rotation. A pitched ball will break in relation to the direction of rotation. The amount of break depends on the speed of rotation (spin) and the velocity of the thrown ball. In most instances, the faster the ball is thrown and the more spin that is generated, the more the ball will break.

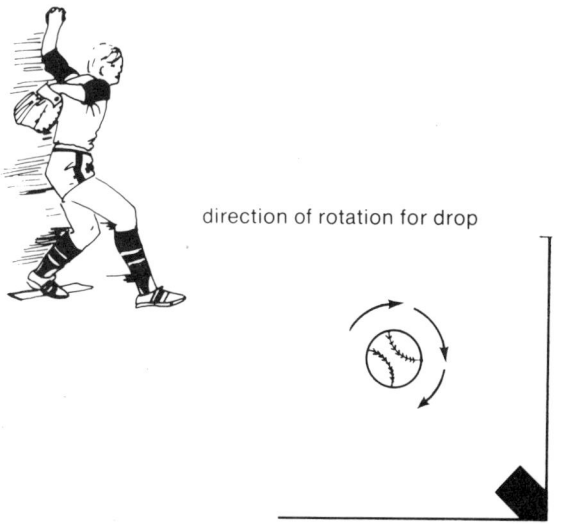

VIEWING THE DROP from third base, the rotation is clockwise.

ONE WAY of gripping drop.

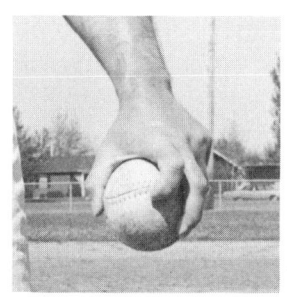

ONE WAY of gripping rise ball.

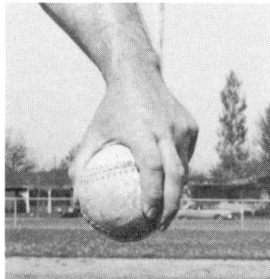

ONE WAY of gripping curve.

ANOTHER WAY of gripping drop.

ANOTHER WAY of gripping rise ball and curve.

DROP BALL

Because of the underhand release, the spin required, and the effect of gravity, the drop should be the easiest softball pitch to learn. Nevertheless, there are many fine pitchers who throw an excellent rise and curve but have never mastered the drop.

In order to obtain the maximum break on the drop, the ball should have a straight downward spin. For example, if you were standing halfway between home plate and third base looking at the pitched ball as a clock, its rotation would be clockwise.

The easiest way to obtain this downward spin is to release the ball with palm facing upward and let the ball roll off the end of your fingers. Most pitchers prefer to hold the ball across the seams with the very tips of the fingers gripping a seam. Some pitchers grip the drop with two fingers, others with three and some with all four.

PITCHING STYLE

DROP SHOULD ROLL off the end of the fingertips.

At the very moment of the release of the drop, the fingers should be parallel to the ground. This parallel positioning of the fingers permits a true downward (top) spin. If the fingers are crooked, you will cause a side spin that will reduce the amount of downward break.

Where to aim the drop depends on who the hitter is, where he is standing in the box, and the count on the hitter. (This strategy will be discussed in a later chapter.) A vast majority of pitchers agree that the drop is most effective when it is thrown from about three inches below to about six inches above the knees. When the pitch is kept in this area, it is very hard for the batter to hit the ball squarely. It should be noted that when the ball is thrown below the knees it is not in the strike zone. However, if it is thrown just below the knees (about three inches), it is very hard for the batter to determine if it is a strike or ball as it approaches. It is a good idea to throw a high drop (just above the waist) occasionally and keep the batter off balance. In fact, the high drop may look like a rise ball coming in, and the batter frequently will take the pitch for a strike.

IN-SHOOT

An in-shoot, or screwball, thrown by a right-handed pitcher will move in toward a right-handed batter. It is thrown in a manner similar to the drop except that the fingers are not parallel to the ground at the time of release. The ball should roll off the fingertips which are placed in a plane vertical to the ground.

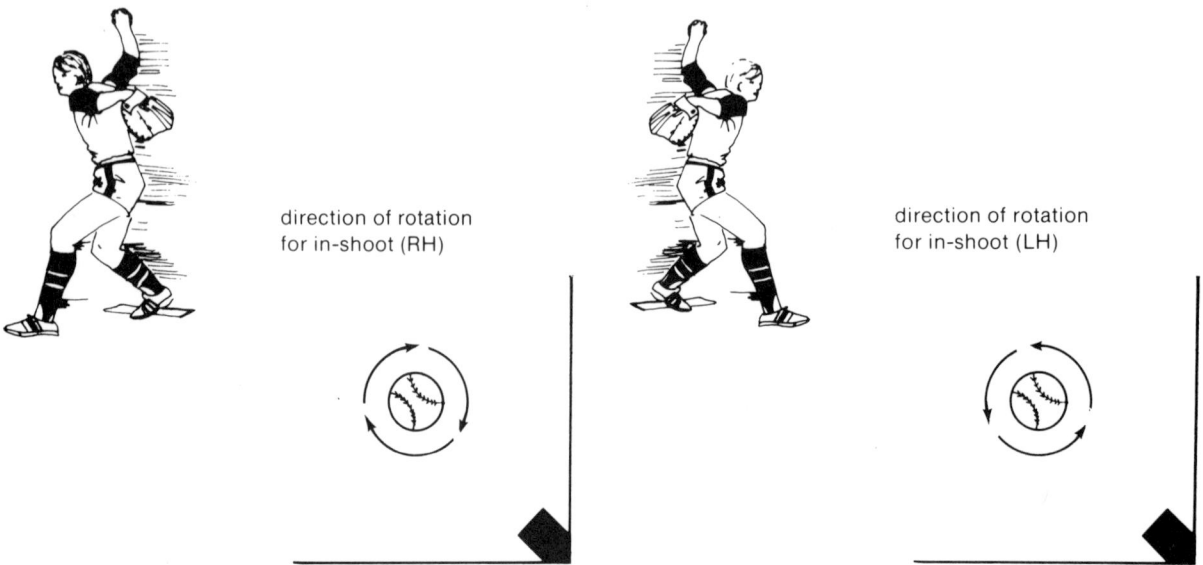

VIEWING THE IN-SHOOT from above the pitcher, the rotation is clockwise for a right-hand pitcher and counterclockwise for a left-hand pitcher.

Usually the in-shoot works best when it is kept low. Of all the pitches, the in-shoot is the most difficult to throw with any consistency.

RISE BALL

The rise ball is really the pitch that provides the softball pitcher with a great advantage over the hitter. A good rise ball, in addition to moving upward, often has a tendency to hop just as it reaches the batter. Even when the hitter times the rise ball accurately, he usually hits under the ball and pops it up.

When the arm is brought forward on the downward portion of the delivery, the wrist should be in a cocked position. A cocked position can best be described in the following manner: hand cupped, wrist bent and extended outward beyond the forearm. Just prior to passing the leg, the wrist is snapped, or turned. Then the forearm, wrist, and hand become a straight line moving parallel to the body. The wrist should continue to rotate on the follow-through motion causing the ball to spin in an upward direction. If you stood halfway between home and third, the rotation of the ball would be counterclockwise. Some refer to this type of rotation as backspin.

There are many ways pitchers grip the ball for the rise. However, the majority use one finger slightly tucked and bent, or they place a knuckle on the seam. Regardless of the grip used, the straighter the vertical rotation the better the ball will rise. If the spin is not a straight backspin, it will tail off and not rise as much. During the early stages of developing stuff, remember that the drop and in shoot should roll off the end of the fingertips. The rise and curve roll off the side or bottom surface of the fingers.

The rise ball is most effective when it is thrown in an area from four to six inches below the armpit to just above the shoulders. Of course the ball is out of the strike zone when it passes above the armpits; but it is difficult for hitters to decide whether or not the pitch will be a strike when it's thrown at the shoulder level.

Although few pitchers can throw a low rise, it is a good pitch to add to your variety of offerings. A low rise is hard to perfect because the pitcher must release it sooner. Consequently, he hasn't the benefit of the longer follow-through motion of the high

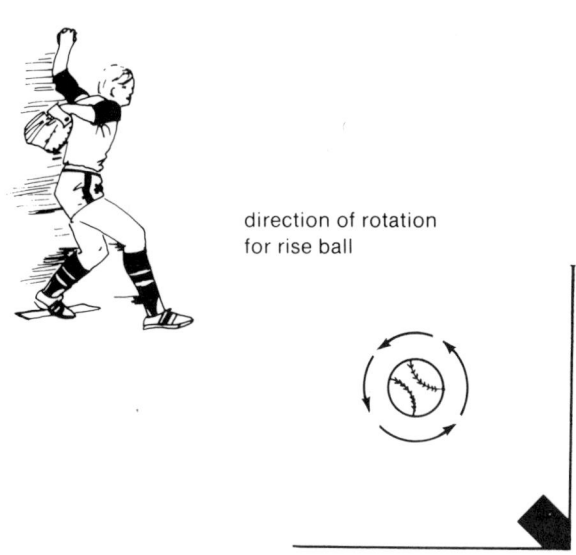

VIEWING THE RISE ball from third base, the rotation is counterclockwise.

RISE AND CURVE ball roll off the side of the fingers.

32 PITCHING STYLE

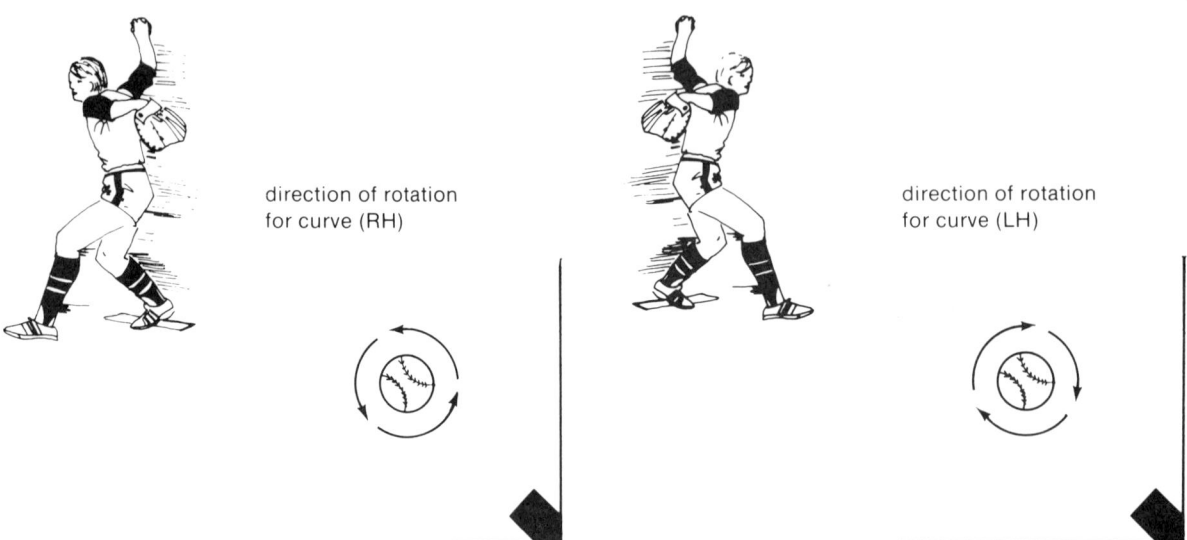

VIEWING THE CURVE from above the pitcher, the rotation is counterclockwise for the right-hand pitcher and clockwise for the left-hand pitcher.

rise ball. A good deal of power must come from the snap of the wrist and elbow. In turn, this places a strain on muscles and ligaments of the forearm, elbow, and shoulder.

A low rise should be thrown in the area from the knee to the crotch. It is a good pitch because it's released so low the hitter expects a drop and takes the pitch.

THE CURVE

For the most part, a curve is gripped and thrown in almost the same manner as the rise ball. The major differences occur in the position of the wrist and follow-through motion. Your wrist must be extended and cupped to a greater degree prior to the release of the ball.

To throw the curve, the wrist must be rotated in a similar manner to throwing the rise. But in the follow-through, the wrist and hand actually move slightly across the front of the body. This motion and release cause the ball to move away from the hitter. If you could suspend yourself above the flight of the pitch, you would see it spinning in a counterclockwise direction from a right-hand pitcher; clockwise from a left-hander.

In order to obtain maximum break on the curve, some pitchers lean with the hip pushed outward. A right-hander will lean to his left while the left-handed pitcher will lean in the opposite direction. This body lean lets the pitcher get the proper rotation without extending the wrist beyond the official limits.

There are two ways of using the curve. First, it can be thrown so that it appears to be heading at the hitter and then breaks across the inside corner. In this instance the intention is to fool the hitter so he'll take the pitch for a strike.

A second approach is to throw the curve toward the center of the plate and break it away from the outside corner. The idea is to get the hitter to swing at the pitch as it breaks away from his reach.

A right-hand pitcher has better luck throwing the curve to a right-hand batter. By the same token, a left-hand pitcher has more success against the left-hand hitter. But when a right-hander throws the curve to a left-hand hitter, the ball is breaking into the plate. It is much easier then for the hitter to pick up the curve.

Most of the leading pitchers do not use the regular curve as often as the rise ball. A regular curve breaks in the same plane. When it is thrown in the middle of the strike zone, it is much easier for a hitter to connect squarely. A combination of the curve and rise, sometimes called the rise-curve, can be very effective. Many pitchers use the rise-curve as their best strikeout pitch.

CHANGE OF PACE

Not all of the great softball pitchers possess a good change of pace (change-up). But many average pitchers become outstanding pitchers when they develop a change-up. A change-of-pace pitch may be a slow drop, slow rise, or slow curve. It may be a combination of some of the pitches previously mentioned. In any case, the change-up is used to keep the hitters off stride. When a hitter knows that a pitcher has a good change-up he is not as likely to "dig in" and take his natural full swing.

The secret to a good change-up is the consistency of the delivery. Your entire delivery and release must be the same as your other pitches. In order to throw a good change-up, you must slow the ball velocity without changing the speed of your regular motion. This is no easy task.

It may take you several years to develop a good change-up. When you feel confident enough to throw a change-up on a ball-three count, you have developed a very good change.

CHANGE-UP DROP

When throwing the change-up drop, the arm must be kept more rigid or stiff than for the regular drop. Instead of snapping the ball with the wrist, the ball is almost pushed out of the hand. The release should be like the fast drop, with the ball rolling off the tips of the fingers.

Since the change-up drop is used to disrupt the hitter's timing, pinpoint control is not essential. But if the pitch is kept below the waist (as it passes over the plate), the hitter is more likely to swing ahead of the ball.

When the change-up is released high, it will appear to the hitter to be above the strike zone. As a result, he will hesitate or hold up on his swing. This hesitation may give the hitter an opportunity to readjust his timing. On the other hand, the high change-up occasionally fools the hitter to the point that he believes the pitch is coming fast and high. Consequently, he takes the pitch, which often drops in for a called strike. After you perfect a good change-up motion, you will be able to determine through experience the best area to throw your particular change-up.

CHANGE-UP CURVE

A change-up curve, or a change-up rise, is usually quite difficult to master. To get the change curve or rise to slow up enough to fool the batter, the rotation of the ball must be fast, yet the forward velocity is slower than the regular curve. This requires more wrist snap and the follow-through is altered more than on any other pitch. Some pitchers practically eliminate the follow-through. This is one exception for not observing the practice of using a smooth follow-through motion.

KNUCKLE BALL

Although the knuckle ball is used successfully in major league baseball, it is rarely used by softball pitchers. The softball is hard to knuckle because of its size. Those softball pitchers who throw the knuckle ball often use it as a change of pace. A knuckle ball is very hard to throw with any amount of speed.

In the case of the knuckle ball, there should be virtually no spin at all. Instead of depending on rotation and speed, the knuckle-ball pitcher uses nature to do the work. Because there is no spin, the movement of the ball is influenced by wind currents. Wind currents, in turn, are influenced by humidity, temperature, and pressure. As a result, the break of the ball is erratic and unpredictable. Due to atmospheric conditions, a knuckle ball may break substantially on a given day, while at other times it moves very little.

The erratic movement of this pitch can prove to be a disadvantage as catchers frequently have a tough time holding on to the knuckle ball. Therefore it is not a good pitch to throw with men on base, particularly third base.

ONE LAST WORD

During the early period of learning to throw stuff, don't be too concerned about your control. Put your concentration on obtaining proper rotation. A good way to tell if you are putting the proper spin on the ball is to seek advice and help. Ask an experienced catcher or pitcher to receive your pitches. By doing this periodically, you will not get into the habit of throwing an improper spin.

It is likely that your pitches won't move very much at first, even when the proper rotation is achieved. Nevertheless, throwing pitches with different spins will often fool hitters enough so they will fail to connect squarely. After weeks, months, or even years of conscientious practice, your pitches will begin to move properly. As you mature and gain more speed along with proper ball spin, these different types of pitches will begin to break sharply.

SLOW PITCH

In fast pitch the batter is at the mercy of the pitcher. But in slow pitch, the reverse is true. The pitcher cannot throw fast and must put an arch on the ball of at least three feet. For all practical purposes, the pitcher in slow pitch has little opportunity to fool the hitter. Furthermore, the delivery is a true underhand toss similar to pitching horseshoes.

About the only way the pitcher can keep the hitter off balance is to vary the height of the arch. As more arch is placed on the pitch, the angle of the bat at contact becomes more severe. A player new to the game of slow pitch finds it very hard to hit the ball squarely when it is thrown with a high arch. Of course the higher the pitcher attempts to arch the ball, the harder it is to throw strikes. Strange as it may seem to fast-pitch players, a ball may be arched in such a manner that it will drop on the plate and still pass through the strike zone.

Although the rules prohibit the pitcher from throwing stuff, he may put backspin on the ball. This is accomplished by releasing the ball with the back of the hand upward (palm down) and rolling the ball off the tips of the fingers.

Once you have learned to throw strikes consistently with a good arch, occasionally throw a pitch with backspin. Eventually you will be able to mix the height of the arch with more backspin, as well as put the ball to the inside or outside of the plate.

USE YOUR regular windup and delivery in warm-up.

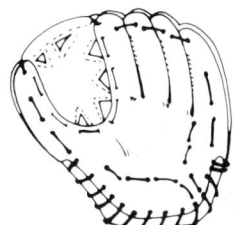

chapter 5
THE COMPLETE PITCHER

Proper attitude development must accompany the physical growth of the maturing pitcher. An even temperament is probably the most important characteristic a pitcher can possess. It's just as necessary to work on reaching good attitude goals as it is to attain good pitching control and improved speed.

It's no easy task to pitch a complete game. Besides the physical strain, certain unexpected things, like an error by a teammate, may have an unfavorable effect on a pitcher. Learning to take an error in stride without letting it affect your concentration is a big step in becoming a first-rate chucker.

Other conditions, such as pinch hitters, the kidding and taunts of opponents, abusive spectator comments, must be met with calm and coolness. At one time or another, a call by an umpire may seem unreasonable at a crucial point in a game. If you can cope with these situations and not allow them to bother your control and rhythm, you will have a much better chance of becoming a consistent winner.

A pitcher who stays cool throughout the entire game and not just in a few rough situations is the most valuable asset a team can have. However, if you lose your head just one time in a rough spot, the game may be lost at that point. Once opposing teams find that a pitcher loses his concentration under pressure, that weakness will be used to an advantage by all of his opponents in future games.

Notice that the word "concentration" is stressed. This ability to keep one's mind focused on performing without being distracted will go a long way in building confidence.

Developing self-confidence can be a difficult task for some, particularly if it isn't in their natural personality makeup. Nevertheless, it is an essential trait you must either have or work hard to strengthen. You must believe in yourself. For example, let's assume you suffer an embarrassing loss and get knocked out of the box in the early innings. Just remember, all pitchers—even the best—sometimes get knocked out of the box. Yet the good ones believe in themselves enough to know that they can pitch against that same team and beat them the next time. That type of confidence must be part of the good pitcher's temperament in order to have a long and successful career.

Last, but certainly not least, desire and dedication are two factors that round out the list of pitching requirements. Reaching any worthwhile goal requires hard work. To become an outstanding softball pitcher is no exception. For many players it means practicing every day for several years in addition to playing in pick-up games, church leagues, park leagues, and organized city leagues before moving up to major softball teams.

Developing the proper attitude, learning to field your position, and throwing an assortment of pitches are major factors in becoming a great pitcher. However, you cannot overlook the finer points of the game, which will be discussed in this chapter.

THE WARM-UP

A proper warm-up routine not only prepares you for each game, but it can help preserve your career. Improper warm-up, either in technique or length of time, may initiate an injury that could be permanent.

Begin your warm-up by first jogging easily. After a few minutes, a couple of short and moderate wind sprints should complete the running portion of the routine. In addition to running, two or three types of calisthenics will further loosen up the wide variety of muscles used in pitching.

How long you spend warming up depends on several factors. For instance, at the beginning of the season a little more time is required to get your muscles performing adequately. Another factor to consider is temperature. On cool nights, more time must be spent in all aspects of the warm-up routine.

I recall a tragic warm-up-related injury that occurred in an Indiana State Tournament. During the time alloted for pre-game workout, a young outfielder rushed to the outfield without warming up. On his first throw to the infield, his arm fractured in two places. There was no fall or impact connected with the injury; it was caused entirely by the throwing motion. He was never able to throw with any power after the accident.

Time will vary with the individual. One pitcher may need 10 minutes, while another may require 20 to 30 minutes. If you take less than 10 minutes, you are inviting trouble.

Unless it is unusually warm, wear a jacket at the beginning portion of the warm-up. Heat generated from your preliminary running is maintained by the jacket and assists in warming up body tissues.

The second portion of the routine consists of the actual pitching aspect. Just as it is important to start running easily, it is equally important to begin throwing in the same way. Your first few pitches should be merely tosses. All muscles—including those of the wrist, forearm, upper arm, and shoulders—are then put into play gradually.

Obviously it is best to warm up with an

WHENEVER POSSIBLE, use an official pitching rubber during warm-up. Keep both feet in contact with rubber.

underhand motion. But an occasional overhand toss assists in getting all muscles of the shoulder and back loosened up. After tossing the ball slowly for a few minutes, begin to throw at half speed without putting any stuff on your pitches. Always make sure that you are at the proper distance if an official pitching rubber and home plate are unavailable. It is a good idea to practice stepping off the official pitching distance, since official warm-up areas are not provided on some fields. Although some pitchers prefer to warm up at long distances, there is absolutely no advantage to this.

Use your regular windup, delivery, and follow-through during warm-up. For some unexplained reason, a number of pitchers take an extra step while warming up. Consequently, they often experience difficulty with their control in the early innings.

When you start to feel comfortable after throwing at half speed, begin to throw stuff—but at moderate speed. Concentrate on one pitch only, and slowly increase speed until you are pitching wide open. Then switch to another pitch, gradually increasing velocity until you are once again throwing at full speed. Follow this pattern with your assortment of stuff. Then you can start mixing the pitches as you would in a regular game.

A regular warm-up routine of this nature will go a long way in preventing injuries such as muscle and ligament pulls. In addition, the pitcher is properly prepared for actual game conditions.

PITCHING STRATEGY

It has often been said that the best philosophy is to overpower the batter; then there is no need to worry about strategy. Sometimes that is exactly what happens. A young, strong pitcher is frequently capable of overpowering the hitter without much concern for what or where he throws.

Even in major competition there have been instances where a young or inexperienced pitcher will throw a no-hitter, strike out 15, walk 10, and lose the game. If such a pitcher shows steady improvement, managers and coaches should not be overly concerned about control. Above all, the pitcher should not be encouraged to sacrifice speed to get the ball in for strikes at this point in his career. Control will come with maturity and more game experience. However, a young pitcher who fails to heed the advice of the coach will find that he will not get by with speed and stuff alone. Sooner or later he must become a thinking pitcher.

KNOW THE HITTER

Practically every hitter has some weakness. To be most effective, a pitcher must exploit a hitter's weakness or weaknesses. Certain hitters are weak on the rise ball, others have trouble with the drop, and some are poor on the change-up. Prior to the start of a game, it is a good idea to go over the opponent's lineup with your catcher and review each hitter's weaknesses and strong points.

Obviously you want to take advantage of the hitter's weak points by throwing the pitch that bothers him the most. But don't get into a rut and throw it every time. Even a weak rise ball hitter will eventually connect if the rise is thrown on every pitch.

Besides having difficulty with a specific type of pitch, a batter often may be weak in a specific area. For example, he may be able to hit an outside drop fairly well but may be very weak on an inside drop. A hitter who pulls may murder an inside rise ball; yet he might have a problem with an outside rise or curve ball.

Crowds the Plate

When a batter crowds the plate there is usually a specific reason. He may be weak on an outside pitch and thus compensates by standing close to home plate. On the other hand, he may have trouble with the inside pitch, and is trying to trick the pitcher into throwing pitches outside.

If you are not familiar with the hitter, it may be necessary to experiment to discover the reason for crowding. Usually, the hitter who crowds the plate is vulnerable to an inside drop, a curve that breaks on the inside corner, or a high, inside rise ball.

Stands Away

A hitter who has difficulty hitting an inside pitch often compensates by standing far away from the plate, where he has a much better chance of connecting squarely with an inside pitch. However, don't fail to exploit a weakness just because a hitter tries to adjust his stance to protect his shortcoming.

In many cases when the hitter adjusts his stance to protect a weakness, he creates other problems for himself. The hitter who stands far away will usually have a problem hitting pitches on the outside corner. This is particularly true with a curve or rise curve that breaks away from the outside corner. He is also weak on a change-up thrown on the outside.

Front of the Box

Hitters who stand in the front portion of the batter's box feel they can hit the ball before it breaks. Although this idea sounds good, it is not usually factual. Theoretically, a low rise, a high drop, and an inside curve are the most effective pitches against this stance. You must also observe where the hitter is standing in relation to the plate—close or far away. A change-up thrown high may also fool the hitter and drop in for a strike. Since he is standing in front of the plate, the ball may pass his shoulders but drop in for a strike as it goes over home plate.

Back of the Box

A hitter who stands deep in the box does so because he believes he has a little longer to look the pitch over. In most cases the low drop, high rise, or an outside curve should be most effective. Many hitters who are weak on the change-up prefer to stand deep in the box. Be careful when throwing a change-up to this type of stance and keep it low.

A low drop that passes by the lowest part of the strike zone of a batter standing even with the plate will pass below the knees of a hitter who stands deep. According to the rules, the strike zone is that space over any part of home plate which is between the batter's arm pits and the top of his knees. Nevertheless, umpires have a tendency to call the pitch in relation to the batter himself rather than where it passes over the plate. (Your catcher should always watch the position the batter takes and point it out to the umpire.)

Pull Hitter

A hitter who pulls (a right-hander who persistently hits to left field or a left-hander who persistently hits to right) meets the ball out in front of the plate. To look at it another way, the pull hitter swings early. A drop, curve, or rise thrown to the outside corner will be the best choice for this kind of hitter. Also, a pull hitter is often weak on the change-up.

Opposite Field Hitter

An opposite field hitter (a right-hander who usually hits to right field or a left-hander who usually hits to left field) swings late. This type of hitter is normally weak on an inside drop or inside rise ball. He is usually not as easily fooled by a change-up as the pull hitter is.

Other Considerations

A smart pitcher takes advantage of individual hitters' faults. Some hitters tend to step away (stepping in the bucket) instead of

A HITTER who strides away from the plate (steps in the bucket) normally is weak on an outside pitch.

HITTERS with a long stride are often poor rise-ball hitters.

striding straight ahead. This type of hitter is usually weak on outside pitches as well as a change-up. The length of the hitter's stride should be closely observed. Those hitters who take an exceptionally long step are often weak on the rise ball.

Remember, these suggestions are based on the average situation and do not apply in every case. You must discover for yourself the weaknesses and strong points of your opponents. But again, don't make the mistake of throwing to his weakness on every pitch. Although that statement was made before, it is an important fact to keep in mind.

You must mix your pitches without developing a habit of pattern pitching. Pattern pitching may be illustrated by the following situation. Let us suppose a hitter is weak on a low inside drop. The pitcher throws a low inside drop on the first pitch; the second pitch is a high outside rise; and the third is a low inside drop, etc. Obviously the pitcher is working on the hitter's weakness and is still mixing his pitches. But if he follows this sequence every time he faces the hitter, he is pattern pitching. Eventually, the hitter will recognize this routine and anticipate what the pitcher is going to throw.

DON'T TIP

The sole reason a pitcher learns to throw a variety of pitches is to fool the hitter. All of this effort may go to waste if the pitcher tips his pitches.

Tipping your pitches means that you do something unusual with your grip, presentation, or windup that permits the hitter to know what pitch you are going to throw. Sometimes this fault is very obvious and may be corrected quickly and easily. On other occasions, the fault could be hard to detect and very difficult to correct.

One of the best ways to determine if you are tipping is to have an experienced coach or player observe your various pitches. Another method is to take moving pictures. In either case, it's best to test yourself during actual game conditions.

Probably the most common way of tipping a pitch is the way you grip the ball. A hitter may be able to see the grip from the batter's box, or a coach may relay a verbal signal to the hitter. This fault can usually be corrected by gripping the ball while it is in

HIDE GRIP well from first- and third-base coaches.

your glove. It may be necessary to keep the glove wrapped around the ball and your hand until you are ready to deliver the pitch. Even though a pitcher may hide the ball well while he gets the proper grip, he may tip the pitch by moving his forearms, elbows, or shoulders in various ways for different pitches.

The presentation is another area where a pitcher often tips. As an example, he may hold the glove vertically on the drop and horizontally on the rise ball. Presenting the ball at different spots for different pitches is another common mistake. Some pitchers hold one type of pitch slightly lower during the presentation pause than they do another type.

Another thing to watch is the height of the pump just after the presentation pause. The height of the pump should be kept the same on every pitch. Look for a variation in the position of your shoulders as you begin your delivery. Some pitchers have a tendency to either raise or drop one shoulder on different pitches. Even your backswing should be checked to see if it remains the same on all pitches.

There are any number of other characteristics a pitcher may develop that will give his pitches away. You, your coaches, and other members of the pitching staff should be alert for these faults.

The concern expressed about tipping pitches may seem trivial to some players. But it should be noted that more than one National Tournament was won because a certain team had the advantage of knowing what the opposing pitchers were throwing.

SLOW PITCH

Although the pitcher in slow pitch need not concentrate on pitching technique to the degree required in fast pitch, he will certainly benefit by following many of the methods described in this chapter. A proper and consistent warm-up routine is very important, even though the throwing time may be reduced. Delivering warm-up pitches at the proper distance will aid the pitcher in throwing strikes in the early innings. Use the same presentation and delivery during the warm-up as you would in actual game conditions.

It is good to know the hitter's weakness in slow pitch, just as in fast pitch. Although the pitcher doesn't have the chance to throw the variety of pitches as in fast pitch, he can aim for certain spots. Pitching strategy differs somewhat in slow pitch. For example, a hitter who pulls the ball normally prefers a pitch inside or across the heart of the plate. In slow pitch, strategy often calls for the pitcher to throw to the hitter's strength. Consequently, by throwing the pitch inside, the batter may pull the ball foul for a strike. He may also hit it on the handle and pop it up. Strategy may also dictate throwing to his power and overshifting the fielders to the direction he normally hits.

These previous comments should not be interpreted to mean that you always pitch to the hitter's strength. Just as in fast pitch, if a hitter has trouble hitting an outside pitch solidly, you should take advantage of that weakness whenever possible.

Even though pitching strategy adds to the effectiveness of the pitcher, his primary asset to the game is his fielding. The pitcher in slow pitch quickly moves backward off the mound after he releases the ball. By throwing the pitch to a specific spot (inside or outside) he can move in the direction he anticipates the hitter will hit the ball.

Too often the importance of the pitcher is overlooked. Not only can he be a valuable asset for his pitching technique, but his fielding contribution can make the difference between an average infield and a very airtight infield unit.

SIGNALS are given in a squat position. Glove hides signals from third-base coach.

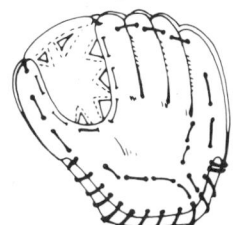

chapter 6
THE CATCHER

There are many reasons why a ball player ends up playing a particular position. A youngster may decide that he wants to be a pitcher and simply works hard and eventually reaches his goal. Others may have been influenced by relatives or their major league hero. Physical characteristics often prove to be a deciding factor. A left-handed thrower is not likely to become a catcher, third baseman, or shortstop. Someone slow on his feet seldom plays shortstop, second base, or center field since those positions require speed and agility.

Many other reasons also enter into the selection of positions. Unfortunately, the most important consideration is often overlooked. Does the player have the physical and mental traits to play a particular position?

TRAITS OF THE CATCHER

Leadership is one of the most important traits to be considered in the selection of a catcher. He usually has sole responsibility for calling the pitches and reminding his teammates how many outs there are. A catcher must have a good memory in order to recall all hitters' strengths and how well his pitcher can handle each hitter.

The catcher should be a take-charge guy who can put some pep into the entire team when it's needed most. He must be able to handle all types of pitchers and react quickly to any change in their performance throughout the game.

Since the catcher is the only one who has a good view of the entire field, he makes sure that all fielders are properly positioned. He also calls out what base should be thrown to on a bunt. In addition, he makes the decision as to when the ball should be cut off on throws from the outfield. Because the catcher is involved on nearly every play in a ball game, he should be a student of the rule book.

There is no strict list of physical abilities or size requirements that must be followed in the selection of a fast-pitch catcher. It does help however, for the player to be strong, tough, and limber. He is the one player in softball who is subject to hard slides at the plate and is often hit by stinging foul tips.

The catcher must have a good, accurate arm. Although a strong arm is nice to have, it is not absolutely necessary. However, to get rid of the ball quickly and accurately is very important. A catcher doesn't need to have good speed, but he must move quickly in any direction. In other words he should have quick reactions.

GIVING THE SIGNAL

A catcher gives signals (signs) to the pitcher with the fingers of his throwing hand. When signals are flashed, the catcher is in nearly a squat position. Knees are spread, with the glove hanging from the left knee. The glove, in this position, hides the signals from the third-base coach. Once a coach steals a signal, it is very easy to relay it to the hitter. And a hitter who knows which pitch is coming has a big advantage.

Without a runner on second base, signals may be kept simple. One finger can mean a drop, two fingers a rise, three fingers a curve, etc. However, when second base is occupied, it is necessary to use a code to prevent the runner from stealing the signals.

There are any number of codes that can be used. One simple way is to use a prearranged series of signals. Another method of doing this is by using a key sign. For example, the first signal flashed is the key which determines what sign in the series is the right one. If one finger is flashed on the first signal (key sign), the pitch wanted will be given on the very next signal in the series. When two fingers are flashed on the first signal (key sign), it means that the intended signal will be given on the second sign after the key.

Just as the pitcher may tip his pitches, a catcher may give away his signals. All signals should be flashed with the fingers placed deep in the crotch area. If the fingers are held too low (below the crotch), the sign will be picked up by either the first- or third-base coach. An unusual movement of the forearm or elbow of the throwing arm while giving signals is another way a catcher may tip his signal. Sometimes a catcher gets into the habit of placing the glove high on the rise and low on the drop when he gives a target, an easy way for the coach to steal the signal.

RECEIVING STANCE is a combination of the crouch and squat positions. A clenched fist helps avoid fractured fingers.

RECEIVING STANCE

Learning the proper stance and becoming comfortable in it is a big step in becoming a good catcher. The stance should be a combination of a crouch and a squat. In this stance, the catcher can stop balls in the dirt, handle high pitches, and move out quickly for a bunt.

The catcher should stand as close to the batter as possible. His feet should be comfortably spread, with the left foot placed slightly ahead of the right, weight on the balls of the feet. This position allows him to move easily in either direction. He is also able to turn quickly for a foul fly, as well as being in a ready position for a throw to any base.

In the beginning, a young catcher tends to stand too far behind the batter. As a result, low pitches that hit in front of him are difficult to handle. Standing too far back is only natural and is due to a fear of being hit by the bat. This fear will be overcome. Through actual game experience, the young catcher gradually becomes relaxed and comfortable standing close to the batter. A few words of caution should be offered at this point. It is possible for the youngster to stand too close since he is not able to judge the proper distance at first. Therefore, careful attention should be given to this problem in the very early stages of instruction.

Another common problem of the beginner is blinking his eyes when the batter swings. For a short while, he will have trouble catching any ball cleanly when the batter swings at a pitch. Again, this problem will disappear through regular practice and playing in games.

RECEIVING THE PITCH

After the signal has been given to the pitcher, the catcher gets into the receiving stance. At this time, the catcher holds his glove up and open, providing a clear target. The throwing hand, with fingers slightly clenched, is held just behind the thumb portion of the glove. Keeping the fingers clenched helps avoid broken fingers from

CATCHER USES body to block a wild pitch that bounces in the dust.

foul tips and wild pitches. As soon as the ball hits the glove, the throwing hand slides over the ball keeping it in the pocket.

With men on base there are two types of pitches that give the catcher the most problem. One is the pitch that bounces in the dirt. If the ball bounces directly in front of him, he usually has a good chance of stopping it. However, the pitch that bounces to the inside or outside of the plate is another matter. Whenever possible, the catcher must try to get in front of the ball, even if he has to dive for it. In this manner his body will keep the ball from going back to the screen.

Another pitch that is hard to handle is one that comes inside and looks like it will hit the batter. The hitter's body screens the ball, and the catcher may temporarily lose sight of the pitch. Again, he must try to keep the ball in front of him by moving quickly to block the ball.

POP FLY

To the average spectator, catching a pop fly near the plate is an easy play to make, but it is more difficult than it seems. As soon as the catcher knows the ball has been popped up, he quickly tears off his mask. At this point he should first get sight of the ball and then throw the mask aside. Otherwise he may stumble on it while chasing the pop fly.

An alert catcher will check the wind direction during the game. Often the pop up is high and the wind can carry it quite far. It's much easier to keep the ball in front of you if you remember the wind direction. Backpedaling after the ball is the reason many pop ups are dropped.

GET SIGHT of the ball before throwing the mask away. Otherwise you may stumble on the mask while going after a pop fly.

PLAYS AT HOME

Probably the most exciting play in softball occurs when a runner is trying to score the winning run with a daring slide at home plate. A runner trying to score will be giving everything he has, and catchers must be prepared to take a hard knock on this type of play.

All of the work and effort put forth in an entire game can depend on one final play at home plate. Making that play correctly is not easy for even the most experienced catcher. Outfield throws to the plate usually come in on a bounce and often take a bad hop. First, the catcher must make a clean catch. At the same time, he must try to watch the runner out of the corner of his eye. A good base runner will watch to see which way the catcher is moving and slide accordingly. A common mistake made by the inexperienced catcher is to completely take his eyes off the ball and look at the runner. Then even if he does catch the ball he probably won't have a good enough grip to hang on to it when he makes the tag.

Whether the runner comes in standing or sliding, the catcher must block the plate. The meaning of "blocking the plate" is the most misunderstood term in softball. Unfortunately, many youngsters as well as many adults believe it means throwing the body in front of home plate. Actually the catcher should have only the glove and ball well out in front of the plate when he makes the tag.

Although some catchers get away with blocking home plate with their body, the practice is very dangerous. Furthermore, the umpire has the right to rule interference and call the runner safe.

It's best to make the tag in a crouch, with the feet straddling the plate. The glove hand, grasping the ball tightly, should be held well in front of the plate and on the ground. This way the runner will slide into the ball and not under it. Since the runner is usually charging hard, most catchers prefer to use the bare hand to help hang on to the ball.

Obviously there are times when the throw comes in late and the catcher has little chance to get set. In such instances he must make the catch and take a swipe at the runner in one quick motion. However, the important thing to remember is to keep your eyes on the ball. Follow it all the way in from the outfield.

WORKING WITH THE INFIELDERS

A catcher is the only infielder who usually runs to catch up with a ground ball. Although the catcher doesn't make a lot of plays on bunts and topped ground balls, when he does the chance is a tough one. He must quickly jump from behind the plate, catch up with the ball, and quickly decide where to throw. Many times it takes a bare-handed scoop, which is not the easiest play to complete and does require practice and experience to do it well. Nevertheless, it's a play that can be learned by the novice catcher and should be covered in early fielding fundamentals.

A catcher is faced with two distinct problems when he attempts to field a bunt. First, he must jump out for the bunt without interfering with the hitter. Ordinarily, there is little chance of interfering with a left-hand batter. However, a right-handed hitter may get a slow start after bunting, and the catcher must beat the hitter out of the box. Otherwise, he must wait until the bunter has started running before making the play. If the hitter beats the catcher out of the box and the catcher then runs into the hitter, the umpire will normally call interference against the catcher. However, if the catcher gets out first and the runner hits the catcher in any manner the call will be against the runner.

Secondly, the catcher must throw to the second baseman moving to cover first and still not hit the runner with the throw. If the runner runs inside the baseline, he should be called out for interfering. This is a difficult call for the umpire to make and he often fails to notice the violation. When a possible bunt situation presents itself, a sharp catcher will remind the umpire to watch the runner on the play. The best way to practice the throw to first is to use an actual runner so the catcher gets used to making the throw as he would in a game.

On a dropped third strike, the catcher has the same problem as with the bunt. In this case the runner is directly in line of the

WHEN TIME permits, catcher moves to inside of diamond to get a better throwing angle to first base.

throw to the first baseman covering. When time allows, the catcher can move to the inside of the diamond to get a better angle to make the throw. Sometimes, however, it is necessary to make the peg to the foul-line side of first base. Again, the best way to work on this play with the first baseman is to use a runner and practice the throw from different spots behind the plate.

The throw to second base on a bunt or topped grounder is a little easier than making the throw to first. On this play, the catcher throws a bit farther but he has a better view of all the players. In addition, the throw is practically the same type he makes when a runner tries to steal. Nevertheless, the catcher must think ahead and determine who is going to cover second base on the play. For example, if a runner is on first base and a possibility of bunt exists, the shortstop will cover second. But if there is a runner on first and a right-hander is up in a hit-away situation, the second baseman will cover on a topped ground ball. Knowing who will cover is very important since the throw may have to be made while the shortstop or second baseman is running toward the bag. A good catcher will always. think about what he will do if he has to make the next play.

Most of the time, the catcher should not try to throw out a runner at third on a topped ground ball. If there is no other play, it's best to hold on to the ball. In this instance, the third baseman will normally be making a try for the ground ball himself and will not be able to get back to cover the bag. It is also unlikely that the shortstop can beat the runner to the base in this case. But if the runner happens to get a late start, then the catcher may have a chance to throw to the shortstop moving over to cover third.

THROWING THE RUNNER OUT

Since fast-pitch rules prevent a runner from

BALL COMING in high is caught with finger portion of glove pointing up.

BALL COMING in low is caught with finger portion pointing down.

leading off prior to an attempted steal, the runner makes his break only after the ball leaves the pitcher's hand. But even so, throwing a runner out requires a quick and accurate peg. A good throw that will catch the runner stealing consists of several different and distinct steps. Each one must be done smoothly and without a hitch.

As soon as the ball leaves the pitcher's hand, the catcher must look at the runner out of the corner of his eye without losing sight of the oncoming pitch. Secondly, he must catch the ball cleanly and with the proper glove placement. A ball that comes in high should be caught with the finger portion of the glove pointing up; finger portion pointed downward on low pitches.

On the next step, the catcher must get the ball out of his glove, cock his arm and step forward with his left foot. The last step is the actual throw to the fielder covering. A throw that arrives slightly to the right of the bag and one to two feet above the ground is ideal for the fielder to make a tag. If the ball is thrown to the left side of the bag, the fielder has to make a backhand stab and still try to make a tag on the runner sliding.

A young catcher should work on each step until he can execute the throw with accuracy and consistency. To adjust to the distance from home to second base (85 feet), the catcher may work by himself by throwing at an open barrel placed on a box. After he becomes accustomed to the distance, it's better to practice under actual game conditions; receive a pitched ball and then throw to a fielder moving to cover the base. A base runner should be used on occasions in order for the catcher to perfect his timing.

PICK OFF PLAY

Since leading off is not permitted in softball, the pitcher is not involved in pickoff plays as in baseball. Picking off a runner is another play where the catcher plays the key role. A catcher has the chance to pick off a runner whenever he is off any base too

A HIGH THROW to second base misses runner stealing.

far. However, the best chance is in a bunt situation. In order to beat the throw at second, the runner moves off first farther than usual as soon as the pitcher releases the ball.

An alert catcher will watch carefully to see how far the runner jumps off first. When he feels there is a good chance to get the runner, he gives the pickoff signal. Since this type of play is not used very often, the signal need not be hidden as well as regular pitching signals. In fact, it should be plain enough that the shortstop, second baseman, first baseman, and right fielder can see it as well as the pitcher. But if there is concern that the opposing team may steal the signal, then it's best for the catcher to hide it. Then the pitcher or shortstop will relay the sign by a verbal code or through some type of hand signal.

The pickoff play begins with the pitcher who must throw a pitchout (a pitch high and outside). Just as in any bunt situation, the first baseman moves in. In the meantime, the second baseman sneaks in behind the runner and covers first base. A quick throw by the catcher can usually nail the runner trying to get back to first.

Two other fielders have key roles to play during the pickoff attempt. The shortstop covers second in case the runner is trapped and heads for second base, while the right fielder backs up first base in the event of a wild throw.

SLOW PITCH

A catcher in slow pitch has fewer responsibilities than the fast-pitch catcher. Since slow-pitch rules do not allow bunting or stealing, the catcher's main defensive job consists of protecting home plate. Because there are more runs scored in slow pitch, this job is an important one.

Although the catcher has fewer defensive plays to make, he can still assume the role of a team leader. As the team leader, his job includes being a "holler guy" and keeping his teammates aware of the count and how many outs there are. It's also up to the catcher to remember where each batter hits most often, and he is in a perfect spot to see that all his players are properly positioned for each hitter.

For all practical purposes, the slow-pitch catcher does not have to have a real good arm or be particularly quick on his feet. In fact, this position is an excellent spot for a big slow man who can hit the ball "a country mile."

A DIVE for the ball is sometimes a must to cut down an extra-base nit.

chapter 7
PLAYING THE INFIELD (PART I)

A good defense is the best offense according to many managers. This statement becomes a reality when one considers the responsibility of the infield in the fast- and slow-pitch game.

Undoubtedly, the foremost requirement of a softball infielder is good reaction time. The infielder in fast pitch and slow pitch must field and throw the ball much more quickly than the baseball infielder. Base-path distances are 60 feet in softball, compared to 90 feet in baseball.

Results of box scores will show that the majority of defensive plays take place in the infield. What the box score won't show is how difficult each particular chance can be. A few plays are high bounces that can be handled by nearly anyone. But most are difficult bounces or spinning grounders. A good infielder must cleanly field all types of chances and throw accurately to the proper base.

STANCE

Before learning anything else, find a comfortable stance that suits you. A semi-crouch with hands on knees or a semi-crouch with your throwing hand in the glove are most common. Another typical stance is the full crouch with both hands extended toward the ground. Feet should be well spread, with your weight on the ball of the foot. This position permits you to move forward, backward, left, or right with little lost motion.

GROUND BALLS

To be able to field ground balls well is one of the skills of softball that is difficult to master. But learning to handle ground balls properly can be accomplished by following several basic steps.

First, when going for a grounder always keep your glove close to the ground.

56 PLAYING THE INFIELD I

INFIELDERS in comfortable and ready crouch.

Coaches and managers should constantly drill the following thought into the infielders mind: Ground balls are caught by bringing the glove from the ground up. In other words, don't put your glove down at the last minute. As soon as you see the ball coming in your direction, get the glove down as quick as you can. By always following this first basic step, you will be able to keep bad hops from going under your glove.

If you are a beginner in the infield, start with slow moving balls hit directly at you. As the ball approaches, cup the glove slightly and let the fingertips actually touch the ground. Allow the ball to roll into the glove and then quickly and firmly clasp the throwing hand over the ball.

Once you become accustomed to fielding slow grounders hit directly at you, start trying to go to your left and right. Keep your glove low just as you did for the balls that were hit at you. Also work on charging the slow hop type of grounders. There are two

SEMI-CROUCH position gives good balance and allows fielder to get down fast on hot grounders.

important rules to remember when fielding any ground ball: 1) If at all possible, get in front of the ball, and 2) always play the ball; don't let it play you.

It is impossible to predict what any grounder will do, so it's doubly important to get in front of the ball. When you reach for a ball, any strange hop can cause it to pass over or around the glove. By getting in front of the ball, even a tricky bounce will hit some part of the body. This positioning prevents the ball from going into the outfield, possibly for extra bases. Of course there are times when the ball is hit so sharply you are unable to get in front of it. On those occasions you must reach or even dive for the ball to make the play.

To play the ball rather than let it play you takes time and practice. Playing the ball means that the fielder moves in and toward a grounder rather than waiting for it to come to him. Waiting for the right bounce sometimes makes it easier to field, but it also may allow the runner to beat the throw.

Beginners will probably have difficulty for a while with balls that are hit to their extreme right or left. This is particularly true for a right-hander going to his right (left-hander to his left) because he must backhand the ball.

Neither a young infielder nor coach should spend much time on difficult plays involving backhand stops, one hand grabs, or leaping catches off line drives. Making difficult fielding moves will be accomplished through practice, physical maturity, and actual game conditions.

Throw Accurately—Not Hard

Along with learning the basic steps of catching ground balls, another area of concern is throwing. Throwing accurately and getting rid of the ball quickly are much more important than throwing hard. Getting rid of the ball quickly and throwing with accuracy involves good footwork as well as proper arm motion. Pivoting and planting the lead foot properly contributes immensely to good throws. In most cases, experienced infielders make the throw with a sidearm or three-quarter motion rather than a true overhand delivery.

During the learning period of fielding and throwing, the young infielder tends to go through several distinct jerky motions. Don't be concerned about this. Eventually, scooping up the ball, pivoting, and planting the lead foot will become one smooth motion.

Trying to get rid of the ball too quickly is as bad as taking too much time. One of the most common mistakes an infielder makes is to try to throw the ball before he has it. Don't look at the runner. Keeping your eye on the ball until it has actually gone into the glove is one way to overcome this error.

When Not to Throw

Knowing when not to throw is just as important as throwing accurately. It doesn't make much sense to try to throw a runner out when it's obvious he has the throw beaten. A throw of this type is usually hurried and wild. A wild throw won't get the runner, and he may advance one, two—or even three bases. If there is any doubt about getting the runner, hold your throw.

Many players fail to realize that when you hold the ball, you have not completely lost the out. For example, the runner may fail to touch the base, or may be called out for leaving a base too soon or interfering on the play. Furthermore, he may be wiped out on a double play later on.

POP-UPS

Even the youngster who has had little playing experience can manage to catch a simple pop fly. But handling rough chances that require running away from the infield and catching the ball over the shoulder is another matter. Only time and practice, accompanied by good coordination, make it possible to handle these tough chances.

With a simple pop-up that can be reached with little running, position yourself directly under it. Keep your eyes on the ball until it settles into your glove. This is more important than how you catch it. While some infielders prefer to catch the pop fly with the hands forming a basket, others catch it with their hands held over their heads. Either way is acceptable.

What you do with the ball after you catch it is nearly as important as catching it. Let's assume you go after a pop fly that carries you into the outfield or into foul territory. If there is a runner on, he may try to take an extra base after the catch. He may also try to bluff you, hoping to draw a long throw. Don't be fooled by a fake. Hold the ball, ready to throw if necessary, and immediately run back into the infield area keeping your eyes on the runner.

RUNNER TRAPPED

Sometimes the runner may go too far off base and become trapped between the bases. If you are out of position after making a difficult play, hold the ball and run directly at the runner. He will have to make a break for one base or another. When he does, you will have a much shorter throw to make.

There are other ways runners are trapped off base. A hitter may try to stretch a single into a double, then suddenly find that he can't make second. Whenever possible, four defensive men should be involved in making the play. In addition to the two

YOUNG PLAYERS should work on rundowns often. Back-up man always protects base.

players who handle the ball on the rundown, two other players should be backing them up.

Regardless of who gets involved in the play, there is one basic fundamental to remember. Neither base, the one the runner rounded or the one he is going to, should be left unprotected.

At some moment, two runners may be trapped off base. This situation results when one runner is trapped and another tries for an extra base during the rundown. For example, while a runner is trapped between first and second base, the runner on third may try to go home.

Let's assume you are the second baseman involved in the rundown between first and second and you see the runner on third breaking for home. If the runner at third has made a definite break for home, you have no choice but to make a quick and accurate throw to the plate. However, if the runner at third is off base trying to draw a throw to third, it is a different matter. Here is another case where it is best to hold the ball. Run the runner clear back to first base, but keep your eyes on the runner at third. Should the runner at third base go off the bag far enough, run directly across the infield until you see which way he is going to make his break. By running across the diamond you will not have to make a long throw and may even be able to tag the runner yourself.

Keep in mind that when two runners are trapped, always go for the lead runner. If there is ever a doubt in your mind whether or not you can get the trapped man, throw to the front base. This way the runner can be forced back to the base he left.

Working on rundowns is good, fundamental practice and can be fun. During a rundown there should be a minimum number of throws. The infielder must learn to fake a throw well so he can fool the runner into stopping his forward movement. This makes the final tag easier.

WHERE TO PLAY

A good infield must work together smoothly as one unit. Every batter will present a different challenge; and each infielder must respond by playing team ball and not just making an individual contribution.

Every infield should have a leader who takes charge. He is responsible for calling out who should catch pop flies. Also, when a tough situation arises, he is the one who gives instructions on how to handle it.

As we previously mentioned, every batter presents a different play situation. But in general, there are three set positions for the fast-pitch infield: 1) regular depth; 2) bunt or cutoff depth; 3) double-play depth.

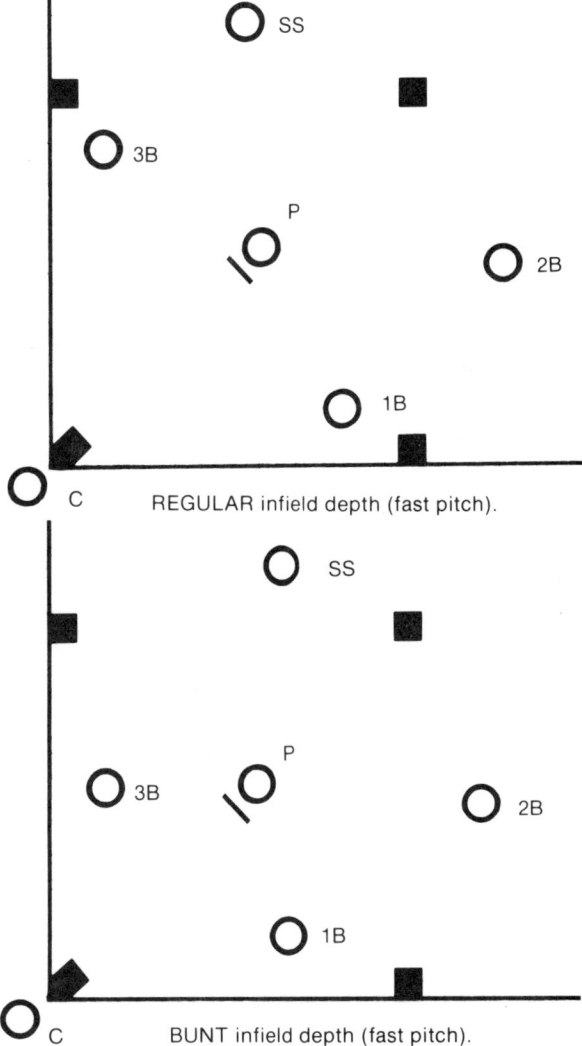

REGULAR infield depth (fast pitch).

BUNT infield depth (fast pitch).

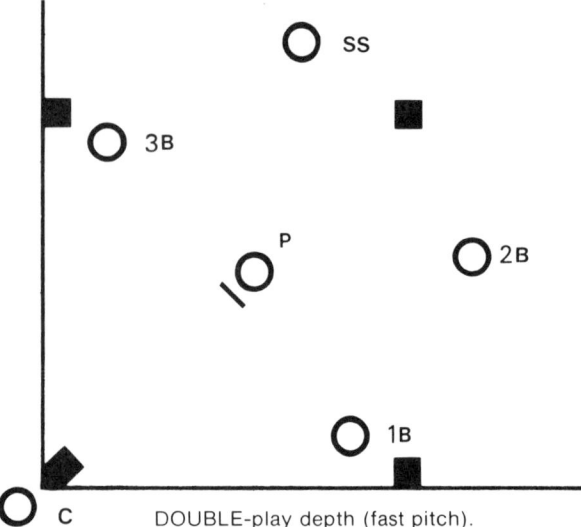

DOUBLE-play depth (fast pitch).

An infield playing regular depth has the first and third baseman from two to five feet in front of the bag. The shortstop and second baseman play from one to three steps in front of the grass and halfway between the bases. In the event there is no grass, the shortstop and second baseman must make a judgment as to where they feel comfortable for taking their positions. Both the shortstop and second baseman will vary their positions from side to side depending on the batter. If the batter is left-handed and a strong pull hitter, the second baseman will play a little deeper and move a few steps toward first. The shortstop will move several steps toward second.

Of course the runner's speed will also cause a slight variation of the regular infield depth. For instance, if a speedy left-hander is up, the third baseman, shortstop, and second baseman will all move in a little.

The double-play depth is used when there is a runner on first or runners on first and second. All infielders draw in several steps, which will cut down on their range somewhat; but this sacrifice is necessary for getting the ball in time to complete the twin killing.

A double play in softball is much harder to complete than in baseball, due to the shorter base paths. This means the first infielder must pick up the ground ball cleanly and make an accurate throw. In turn, the second infielder must catch the ball and make another accurate throw. A third fielder must make a clean catch before a second runner reaches the bag. All this action must be completed within three to four seconds.

The third fundamental infield position is used to cut off a run at home or to play the bunt. All infielders are drawn in very close with the third and first baseman right on top of the hitter.

PLAYING THE BUNT

With first base occupied, the responsibility of the infield in a bunt situation is pretty clear. As the ball leaves the pitcher's hands, the third and first basemen charge toward the plate. As the batter squares to bunt, the second baseman moves to cover first base while the shortstop moves to cover second base. The shortstop must be particularly aware of covering the center portion of the infield in case the hitter fakes the bunt and swings away.

Once the batter drops the bunt fair, it is the responsibility of the catcher to judge where the play should be made. As the infielder reaches to pick up the ball, the catcher must make the call quickly and firmly. If he feels the play can be made at second, the catcher shouts "second base." Whoever fields the ball then pivots and throws to the shortstop, covering second base.

PLAY AT SECOND

When the play is made at second base, there are defensive moves that must be made immediately. Suppose either the catcher, pitcher, or first baseman makes the play. Then the third baseman must move quickly back to cover third. This move is made in case the ball is thrown poorly and the runner tries for third. The pitcher must

AS THE INFIELDER reaches for the bunted ball, the catcher is calling out the proper base.

cover third if the third baseman makes the play. Outfielders also must share defensive responsibility on the play at second. All outfielders must move in and toward second in case of an overthrow.

PLAY AT FIRST

Should the catcher decide the play must be made at first, the infielder scoops up the ball and throws to the second baseman covering first. As soon as the shortstop sees the play is going to be made at first, he moves immediately to cover third base. A fast runner heading for second will often try to keep going, especially if he thinks third base is unprotected. The third baseman must also get back to third should the catcher, pitcher, or first baseman field the bunt.

Whenever the third baseman makes the play, he is not likely to be able to get back to third. The pitcher must then move toward third to help in case the shortstop fails to get there. Outfielders, particularly the right fielder, must move in to back up any wild throws.

FIRST AND SECOND OCCUPIED

One of the most difficult plays to defense occurs when the bunt is used with runners on first and second. The third and first basemen charge home plate, and the second baseman moves to cover first. Which base the shortstop covers depends on several things.

Normally the shortstop moves to cover third; second is left unprotected. Nevertheless, the manager or team captain may elect to have the shortstop cover second and leave third uncovered. The decision as to which base the shortstop will cover should be made before the hitter gets in the batter's box. Two things that may influence the choice of which base to cover are the speed of the runners on first and second, and the hitter's ability to bunt.

With a man on second base only, the decision on what base to cover is much easier. Again the first and third basemen charge home plate, the second baseman covers first, and the shortstop covers third. Frequently, the throw to third must be made while the shortstop is on the run. A play of this type is not easy and must be practiced often before the infielders can execute it well. Prime responsibility for backing up the throw falls on the left infielder.

THE SQUEEZE

With a runner on third base, the offensive team may try the squeeze bunt. On the squeeze play the runner leaves third and heads for the plate as soon as the pitcher releases the ball. It's almost impossible to get the runner on a squeeze play, providing the hitter lays down a good bunt. Nevertheless, a good team always gives its best on every play. Both the third and first basemen must come in quickly and attempt to scoop up the ball on the run. The scoop and underhand toss should be one smooth motion.

A squeeze bunt is usually attempted with at least one base empty. Then the play at the plate is not a force-out so the runner must be tagged.

When the defensive team suspects a squeeze bunt, the shortstop has a choice of covering second or third. There are two major reasons for covering third base: 1) If the hitter pops up, a double play is possible.

RUN SCORES on squeeze bunt.

2) If the hitter bunts the ball too hard, the runner may be trapped between third and home. When first base is unoccupied there is no reason for the shortstop to cover second, so he automatically moves to cover third.

SLOW PITCH

Slow pitch calls for the following three basic infield positions: 1) regular depth; 2) double-play depth; 3) tight infield depth.

Regular infield depth in slow pitch is different from fast pitch. Since bunting is not permitted, both the third and first basemen play deep. They play even with the bag or slightly behind it, depending on the hitter. In the case of a hard-hitting right-hander who pulls, the third baseman will move behind the bag and close to the foul line.

Because of the many hard shots that are hit in slow pitch, the shortstop and second basemen play very deep. For example, when a right-hander is up at bat, the shortstop is usually standing at the edge of the grass. This position gives him the chance to cover short pop flies to the outfield as well as handling hard, hot grounders to his left and right.

Double-play depth calls for the entire infield to draw in. However, the third and first basemen do not come in as close as they would in fast pitch. The shortstop and second baseman move in five or six steps from "regular depth" in order to get to the ball more quickly for the double play.

The only time the infield plays the tight depth is when a runner is on third and represents the tying or winning run. At this time, the first and third basemen come in about three to five feet from regular infield depth. In addition to moving in toward home plate they also move a step or two toward the pitching mound. The shortstop and second baseman are in line with the base paths and closer to second base than they would be in a regular infield depth.

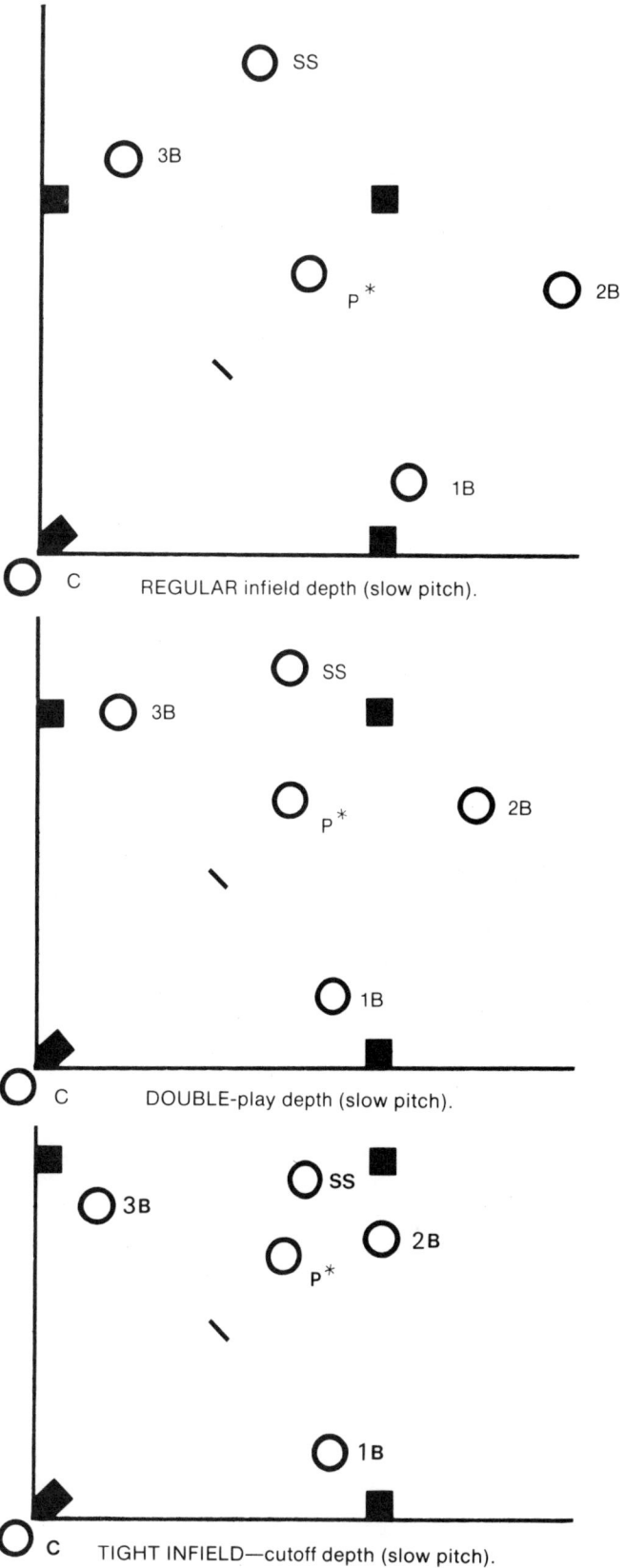

REGULAR infield depth (slow pitch).

DOUBLE-play depth (slow pitch).

TIGHT INFIELD—cutoff depth (slow pitch).

* Pitcher moves back off mound after releasing ball.

FIRST BASEMAN ready to receive throw. Left-handed first baseman stretches with left leg.

chapter 8
PLAYING THE INFIELD (PART II)

FIRST BASE—FAST PITCH

Playing first base in fast pitch requires an alert, sure-handed, and quick-thinking individual. Other than the catcher and pitcher, no other player handles the ball more often. A first baseman has to be ready at all times for a bunt which means he is pulled in close, yet he must also handle the sharply hit ground balls or line drives. It's not absolutely necessary, but it's a definite advantage to be left-handed and tall for playing first base.

Taking the Throw

Whether it's fast or slow pitch, receiving the throw at first requires practically the same moves. The main difference is that in fast pitch the fielder usually turns and runs back to the bag, while the slow-pitch player runs in toward the base. As soon as a ground ball is hit to another fielder, the first baseman quickly moves to the bag. Getting back to the bag is one of the most difficult plays a fast-pitch first baseman makes. Since he usually plays close, he has to turn, run, and be in position in a matter of a couple of seconds. As soon as he reaches the bag, he faces the infielder who has fielded the ground ball and straddles the base. Once he determines the height and direction of the oncoming throw, he can place his feet accordingly. If the first baseman is left-handed and the ball comes to his right, he stretches out with his right foot, while the left foot touches the outfield corner of the bag. If the ball is to his left, he touches the infield side corner of the bag. A right-handed first baseman simply reverses this footwork action. Shifting his feet in this manner gives a first baseman the greatest possible reach.

Some first basemen prefer placing one foot on the bag right away rather than shifting to different corners of the base. Either way is acceptable. However, a common mistake made by inexperienced first basemen is to stay on the bag and try to stretch too far for wide or high throws. If there is any doubt about whether or not the throw can be reached comfortably, you must come off the base and stop the ball rather

RIGHT-HANDED first baseman touches inside corner of bag with right foot and stretches with left leg.

than try to make a spectacular catch. When a throw pulls the first baseman off the bag toward the infield side of the base, he still has a good chance to get the out by tagging the runner.

With runners on base, a first baseman should be particularly alert after the out is made at first. As soon as the catch is made, come off the bag ready to throw.

Don't turn and look at the umpire to see what call he made. Games are lost because the first baseman goes to sleep for only a second or begins an argument with the umpire on the call. Not only can a runner score from third, but a speedy runner may score all the way from second.

Where to Play

Practically every hitter in a fast-pitch lineup is a possible bunter. Therefore, the first baseman must play in close regardless of the hitter's reputation as a bunter. When there are no runners on base and no strikes on the batter, a first baseman plays approximately eight to ten feet in front of the bag. After two strikes he can move back, since there is then less chance the hitter will bunt. As in baseball, the batter is called out if he bunts foul on the third strike.

When an obvious bunt situation arises, the first and third basemen move in until they are within ten to fifteen feet of the hitter. Playing this close is absolutely necessary in order to make the play in time. Once the bunt is down, the catcher will shout loudly to what base the peg should go. If the play is at second, the first baseman

FIRST BASEMAN must always be alert for pickoff throw from catcher.

whips the ball to the shortstop covering. It's a definite advantage to be left-handed on this type of play. A left-hander can scoop up the ball and throw directly across his body. A right-hander must make a half turn or a full pivot to complete the play.

When the play is at first, the throw is made to the second baseman covering the bag. The throw should go to the infield side of the base, otherwise it may hit the runner or cause the second baseman to collide with the runner as he reaches for the throw.

Whenever possible, a good fast-pitch team will always try to get the runner at second on the bunt attempt. A bunt that goes directly to the first or third baseman can even result in a double play. The play is completed by the first baseman, who first throws to the shortstop who, in turn, fires to the second baseman covering first.

One of the toughest defensive moves for a first baseman occurs when the bunt is dropped with a man on first and second. If the play is at third, he must throw past the pitcher to the shortstop moving over to cover third. A bad throw means that at least one run will score, and maybe two. Unless you have a sure out at third, it's best to take the out at first.

Batter Hitting Away

When there are one or two outs and no one on base, the first baseman can afford to play a little deeper than usual. This is particularly true if a right-hand batter is up. However, with a speedy left-hand hitter at the plate, you must play close, in case he tries a drag bunt.

A slow topped ground ball that heads between the first and second basemen should be taken by the first baseman whenever possible. Because he plays in close, the first baseman can get to the ball quicker than the second baseman, who will cover first. In fast pitch, unlike baseball, the pitcher rarely covers first.

With less than two outs and a runner on first, the first baseman must be alert for a possible double play on hard-hit ground balls. Even though he and the other infielders may be drawn in close for a possible bunt, the double play can be made. When the batter hits a hot grounder to him, he fires the ball to the shortstop covering second. The first baseman then hustles back to first base to take the return throw from the shortstop to complete the double play. In some instances the first baseman may be in so close he is unable to get back fast enough to cover first after the throw. An alert second baseman will notice this and rush over to cover the bag.

When runners are on first and second, the first baseman must quickly make a decision whether to throw to third, second, or take the out himself at first. Who will be covering third on the play depends a great deal on how many are out. With nobody out, the infield will be drawn in for a possible bunt, so the shortstop will usually cover third. However, if there is one out the third baseman will be playing a little deeper and he will cover third.

On a very rare occasion, the double play may be made with the first baseman touching first and then throwing to second. But remember, the runner heading for second base must be tagged, since it is no longer a force play. This can happen if the runner on first is slow and the hitter is very fast. The first baseman makes the decision that he will get the fast man for sure and still have time to get the slow man going to second base.

A first baseman is a key man on a base hit to the outfield when one or more runners are on base. As soon as he sees the ball pass through the infield, he gets into position to back up the throw. This is one instance where there is no set place for the first baseman to be. He should be allowed to use his own judgment as to where he can do the best job of backing up the throw. I recall very clearly a play in a National Tournament in which a first baseman backed up a throw at third base and made a game-saving throw to home plate.

FIRST BASE—SLOW PITCH

A big, hard-hitting player with quick hands will find first base an ideal position. And since he does not have to cover bunts, he does not have to be a speedy runner.

A first baseman's main defensive concern is handling throws from the infielders. Nearly all of the fielding suggestions given in the previous material for the fast-pitch first baseman also apply for slow pitch.

Instead of playing eight to ten feet in front of the bag, as in fast pitch, the first baseman plays even with first base or several steps behind it. This way he has a better chance of getting hard ground balls hit to his right.

Slow pitch rules state that a runner cannot leave the base until the ball reaches home plate. As a result, the chance of completing the double play is very good. Because there are many hits and a lot of base runners in slow pitch, it is doubly important that the first baseman be a good fielder with a fine arm.

SECOND BASE—FAST PITCH

A second baseman in fast pitch must be the most versatile player on the team. Of all the infielders he must be the most alert and make the most decisions. A good second baseman should have the following capabilities:

- quick on his feet
- good, accurate arm
- extremely alert, quick reactions
- good fielder, quick hands

The second baseman is responsible for:

- covering first on bunts
- fielding pop flys between infield and outfield
- covering second base on the steal
- covering second base on infield first plays
- covering second base on double plays
- covering second base on throws from outfield
- backing up throws from outfield
- taking cutoff throws from outfield

Covering first base on a bunt is the main job of the fast-pitch second baseman. In a bunt situation, the second baseman

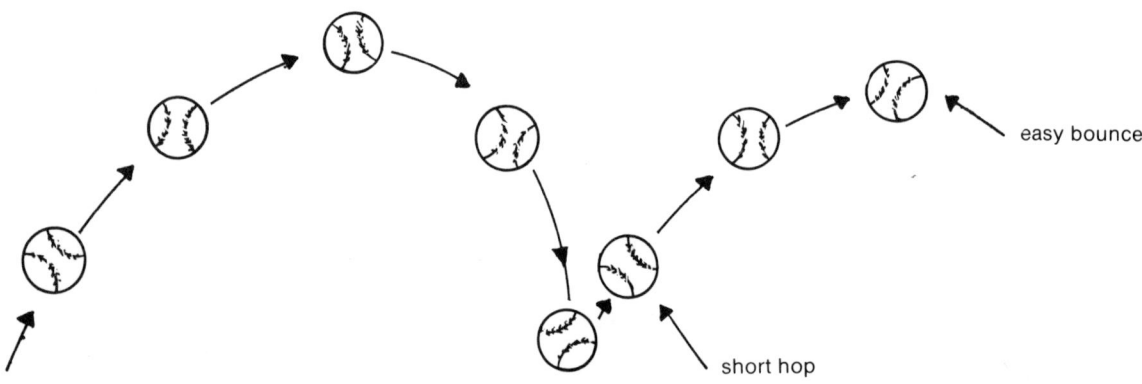

INFIELDERS MUST often take the ball on the short hop rather than wait for the easy bounce.

"cheats" (moves closer to the base) a few steps toward first. Once he sees the batter square around to bunt, he takes a couple of steps closer to first, keeping his eyes on the hitter. As soon as he sees the bunt is down, he continues to first and looks for the throw from either the catcher, pitcher, first, or third basemen.

Both the second baseman and shortstop have far more ground to cover than the first and third basemen. A second baseman has to be fast and be able to get rid of the ball quicker than any other infielder. Although the shortstop and third baseman make longer throws, the ones made by the second baseman are more difficult.

On balls hit to his extreme left, the second baseman often has to throw off balance. In some instances he has no time to stop and must make a backhand, snap throw in order to get the runner. When a ball is hit to his extreme left with a man on first, the best choice is to throw to first for the out. It is almost impossible for the second baseman to go to his extreme left, stop, and throw accurately back to second base in time to get the runner.

Balls hit to your extreme right must be handled with a backhand stop. After the catch you have the following choices: 1) come to a stop, plant your feet, and throw to first; 2) while still running, jump, turn, and throw back to first; 3) hold the ball; or 4) whip the ball to the shortstop and let him make the throw to first. It's rare to use choice number four but it is an option to be considered.

On balls hit to your extreme right with a runner on first base you have the following choices: 1) try to get the runner at second by touching the bag yourself; 2) toss the ball to the shortstop covering second; or 3) hold the ball if there is little chance of getting the runner at second. Unless the ball is hit very hard and the hitter is a very slow runner, throwing back to first is risky. A bad throw may give the lead runner a chance to score all the way from second base.

Slow, chopped ground balls that are out of reach of the first baseman and pitcher must be charged by the second baseman. Grounders like these are often taken on the short hop (a ball bouncing directly in front of the fielder) rather than waiting for the easy bounce. Other than basic fielding instructions and practice and more practice, there is little that can be done to help the beginner. This is a difficult play for even the most experienced player. There is no room for a momentary "bobble." You either make it on the first try or the runner is safe. On a slow spinning ball that hugs the ground, the second baseman may choose to use a bare-hand pickup in order to save time.

The Double Play

Second base is called the "keystone" sack, and indeed it is. More crucial plays are made at second than at any other base, including home plate. And one of the most crucial and interesting is the double play. There is nothing more entertaining than watching a good "keystone combination" (second baseman and shortstop) complete a "twin killing."

The key move is the throw to the fielder covering the bag. It is this throw that either makes or breaks the play. If the throw is too early the fielder covering may not be ready; if it's too low he may drop it; if it's too high or wide it may pull him off the bag; and if it's late he may have passed over the bag. An ideal throw reaches the fielder covering the base about one or two steps before he hits the bag.

When the ball is hit toward the third baseman or shortstop on a double-play situation, the second baseman starts toward the bag immediately. In this case, the throw should hit him on the pitcher's side of second, not the outfield side.

PROPER HEIGHT of throw to shortshop on double play.

SHORTSTOP steps over bag with left foot and drags right foot over bag for force-out and is in position for throw to first.

When the ball is hit directly at the second baseman, or slightly to his left, he makes the regular sidearm peg, hitting the shortstop waist- to letter-high just before he reaches second base. On a ball hit to the extreme right of the second baseman, the short throw is usually handled much easier if it is an underhand toss. In some instances the ground ball may pass so close to the second baseman that he can make the pickup and touch the base himself.

There is a difference of opinion among players and coaches as to what foot should touch the bag on a force-out at second. Some contend so many things affect the play that it is not practical to hit the base with any particular foot each time. One recommended way is to take the throw before reaching the bag and step over it with your left foot. As you pass over the bag the right foot is lightly dragged across it. In this manner you are ready to throw to first and you have left the baseline clear for the runner.

Throws from the Catcher

Covering second on the steal attempt is another key responsibility of the second baseman. Normally, the second baseman covers the bag when a right-hand hitter is up. The shortstop covers with a left-hander at bat. However, this is not a fast, hard rule. In some cases the situation will be reversed, and the second baseman will cover with a left-hander at bat. A good infield combination will have hand signals or verbal codes that determine which man will cover second base on each play.

TAG IS MADE by letting runner slide into ball.

Three distinct moves with near-perfect timing have to be made in order to complete the tag play at second. First, the fielder must get a quick start to the base. A slow start or any slight hesitation means the runner will be safe. Keeping a close eye on the runner on every pitch is the key to getting a head start. As soon as the second baseman sees the runner is taking off, he heads for the bag. While running, he watches for the throw instead of arriving at the bag and then looking for it.

The second key move is to catch the ball cleanly whether it's high, low, wide, or in the dirt. At this point you cannot afford to take your eye off the ball for a second. One little peek at the base or runner may mean a dropped or fumbled throw. Moving from the catch to the tag should be one continuous smooth motion. An experienced fielder makes a one-hand catch and drops the glove to the ground in front of the bag letting the runner slide into the ball. Younger players should make a two-handed catch until they are able to handle the one-hand tag comfortably.

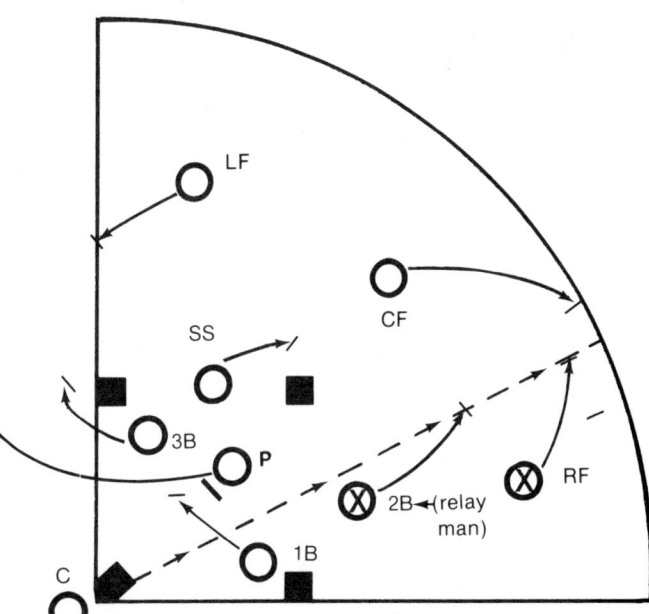

MOVEMENT OF FIELDERS for relay on extra-base hit to right field. Right fielder retrieves ball and throws to second baseman (fast pitch).

Outfield Relays

As soon as a base hit goes into right or right center, the second baseman moves into short right or short-right center field, depending on where the hit goes. On long extra-base hits, the second baseman will relay the ball to third or home. Either the first baseman or shortstop will tell the second baseman where the ball should be thrown.

If the relay throw is fairly long, it's best to throw the ball into third or home on one hop. A throw that bounces once on its flight is a little easier to handle. But if the relay is a short throw, a good line-drive type peg will get to the base a little quicker than the one-bounce throw.

SECOND BASE—SLOW PITCH

A second baseman in slow pitch does not have to worry about covering first on bunts or protecting second on steals. But he does have to make all the rest of the difficult fielding plays required of a fast-pitch second baseman. And in addition, he has to make them much more often in a game.

Because there are many more hard-hit balls in slow pitch, the second baseman plays deeper than the fast-pitch second baseman. Besides handling blistering ground balls and line drives, his job includes fielding many short pop flys (texas leaguers) that are hit between the infield and outfield.

The second baseman and shortstop are the key to a strong infield unit. In fact, trying to field a slow-pitch team with an average second baseman and shortstop is like fielding a fast-pitch team with a mediocre pitcher... it means trouble.

SHORTSTOP—FAST PITCH

In many ways, the shortstop and second baseman have the same responsibilities. And both the shortstop and second-base positions require players with similar physical and mental capabilities. Since these capabilities were previously discussed, they will not be repeated. This is one position where a good strong arm is very essential, as the shortstop makes the longest throws of any infielder.

One of the most difficult plays the shortstop makes occurs when he has to go deep in the hole (between shortstop and third base) to field a ground ball. It usually requires a backhand stop and a long hard throw to get the runner at first base. A throw of this distance ordinarily requires an overhand peg, one of the few times an infield throw is not a sidearm motion.

With nobody on, the shortstop normally plays fairly deep. In this position he can cover most ground balls hit to his extreme right or left, as well as short pop flys to short center and left field. An exception to playing in this spot may happen when a very speedy left-hand batter is up. In this case, the shortstop will move in a few steps in order to get to a ground ball quicker.

When a runner is on first with no out, the shortstop has several fielding possibilities: 1) cover second if the batter bunts; 2) cover second in case of an attempted steal; 3) cover second if the ball is grounded to the first or second baseman; and 4) field a ball if it is hit in his direction.

With an obvious bunt situation present, the shortstop cheats and takes a position a little closer to second than usual. If the batter squares to bunt, the shortstop starts for second but keeps his eyes glued to the hitter. Some hitters fake a bunt and then swing away. Once the bunt is down, the shortstop moves quickly to cover second base. A bunted ball that is fielded immediately will probably be thrown to the shortstop covering second. The shortstop takes the throw on the run, tags the bag and if possible, whips the ball to first base for the double play. It's not often a double play is completed on a sacrifice bunt, but it is a play to be considered at all times.

On a bunt play where the throw is made to first base, the shortstop has an added responsibility. Once he sees that the throw is not coming to second, he quickly moves to cover third. Otherwise, third base may be left unguarded, since the third baseman always moves in to field the bunt.

Catching the Base Thief

According to the book, the shortstop covers second on a steal when a left-hand batter is up; the second baseman covers with a right-hander batting. However, let's assume a right-hander is at bat with a runner on first and nobody out. In addition to being a good spot for a steal, it's also an excellent time for a bunt. Consequently, the second baseman will be cheating a little toward first and will have a hard time making it to second base if the runner tries to steal. In this instance, the second baseman and the shortstop will get together or give a signal as to who will cover on the steal. A good share of the time the shortstop covers second on the steal in this situation.

A shortstop has his hands full when there are runners on first and second and nobody out. First of all, he must cover third on either the bunt or an attempted double steal. On this play the shortstop moves in a little and cheats toward third, and the second baseman cheats toward first. As a result, the center position of the infield is wide open. If the batter pokes a ground ball up the center of the infield, the shortstop has a lot of ground to cover to reach the ball.

Double Play

Handling the throw on the double play is usually easier for the shortstop than for a second baseman. While the second baseman must touch the bag and pivot before throwing back to first, a shortstop is running in the direction he is going to throw.

On the double play, a good throw will get to the shortstop about one to two steps behind (the outfield side) second base. He then steps over the bag with his left foot, and the right foot drags lightly across it as he makes a quick snap throw to first base.

Runner on Second Only

With a runner on second only and less than two outs, the shortstop faces one of his toughest challenges. He must cover third on a bunt or a steal; and if the play is there he has to tag the runner, since it is not a force play. Although the third baseman may be able to cover third on a regular steal, it seldom happens. Most of the time, a good team will fake a bunt and then have the runner steal. By faking the bunt, the third baseman is pulled out of position and the shortstop must cover third.

In this same situation, a ground ball hit to the shortstop presents a couple of problems. On a slow hopper, he must field the ball without interfering with the runner. However, if he has a chance to get to the ball first and the runner hits him, the runner is called out for interference. Some of the more clever and quick-thinking shortstops will lightly bump a runner intentionally if they feel they cannot make the play, hoping to make it look like runner interference. In some cases they get away with it.

Again, in this same situation, when the shortstop fields a hard-hit ground ball, he must quickly determine if he can tag the runner. If not, and if the runner has had time to break for third, he must make up his mind whether or not he can get the runner at third. Remember, this is not a force play and requires that the runner be tagged. Sometimes the ball is hit so hard the runner has barely got off the bag. In this case, the shortstop should force the runner back to second and throw to first for the out.

Outfield Relay

We mentioned earlier that the second baseman is the relay man on long hits to right field. The shortstop is the relay man on long and extra-base hits to left and center field. Once the shortstop sees that a hit to left or center field will likely go for extra bases, he moves out to short left or short center field. With his back to the infield, he calls for the ball to be thrown to him. Just before the shortstop catches the throw, another infielder (usually the second baseman) will

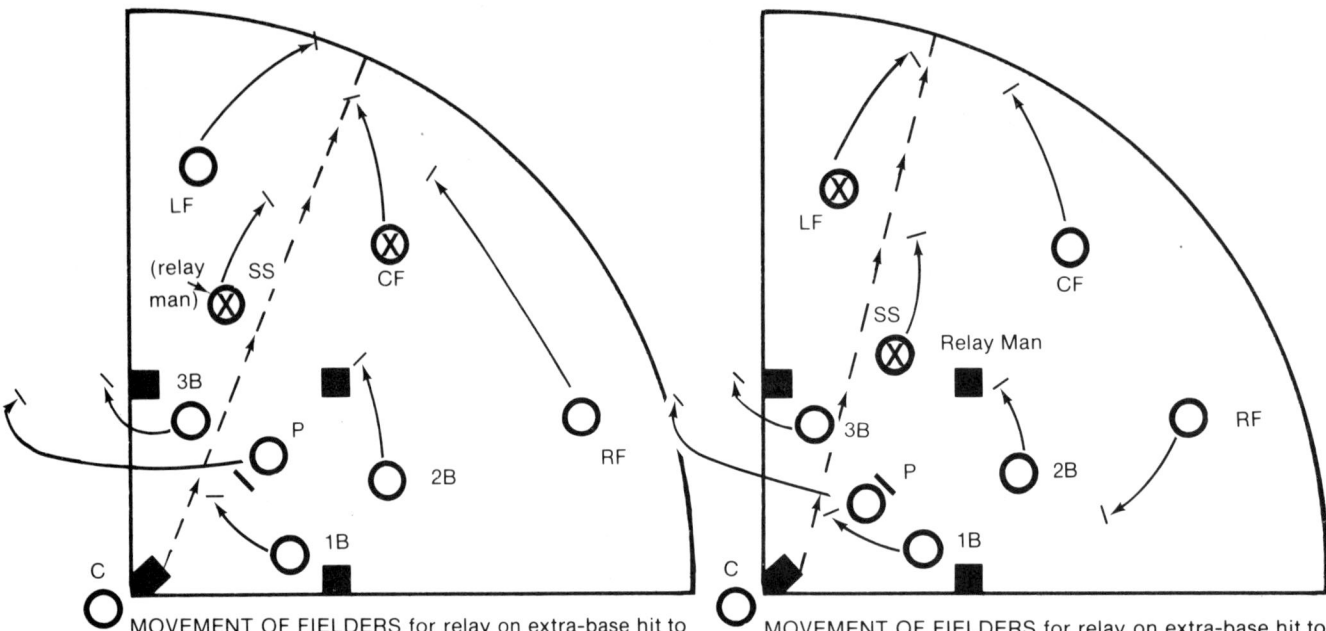

MOVEMENT OF FIELDERS for relay on extra-base hit to center field. Center fielder retrieves ball and throws to shortstop (fast pitch).

MOVEMENT OF FIELDERS for relay on extra-base hit to left field. Left fielder retrieves ball and throws to shortstop. (Fast pitch)

call out the base where the throw should go. If the throw is supposed to go to third, it will be a fairly short one and should be thrown on the fly. But if the throw goes to home, a one-bounce peg will be easier for the catcher to handle. The one-bounce peg should hit at least ten to twelve feet in front of the catcher.

SHORTSTOP—SLOW PITCH

To be an outstanding slow-pitch shortstop, a player must be a gazelle and have an arm like a cannon. Although this statement is a slight exaggeration, the shortstop has a tremendous amount of ground to cover. Furthermore, he has by far the longest throws to make of any infielder. Because the outfield fences are longer from home plate in slow pitch, the outfielders play deeper. As a result, the shortstop plays deeper in the infield in order to get the short outfield pop flys.

A strong arm is an advantage, but throwing accuracy and the ability to get rid of the ball quickly is just as important. A shortstop who is a good fielder and has a strong arm but who frequently throws wild is more of a liability than an asset.

OUTFIELD RELAYS

Most slow-pitch teams now play with four deep outfielders instead of three deep outfielders and one shortfielder. Because of this, the importance of the shortstop and second baseman as relay men has increased greatly. A shortstop and second baseman may make several relay throws in a game. Working on the relay throw is an exercise that should be part of every practice session for the experienced as well as the beginner.

THIRD BASE—FAST PITCH

Third base has always been referred to as the hot corner because of bullet-like shots hit at the third baseman. Although the third baseman in fast pitch must contend with line shots, his main job is fielding bunts and topped ground balls.

A third baseman should be able to move like a cat and have quick hands. Because the shortstop plays deep, slow topped ground balls should be taken by the third baseman whenever possible. This means the third baseman must be able to move to his left very fast, make the stop and get rid of the ball in one quick, smooth motion.

THIRD AND first baseman play well in front of bag in fast pitch.

Where to Play

A fast-pitch third baseman plays closer than any other infielder. Unless a slow running, hard-hitting right-hand batter is up, his normal position is ten to twelve feet in front of the bag. On a bunt situation, he plays only twelve to fifteen feet from the hitter and cheats a little toward the pitcher's mound.

Whenever possible the third baseman will try to get the runner at second on a bunt. As soon as he reaches for the bunted ball, the catcher calls out "first" or "second" base. If the runner is forced out at second, the third baseman's job is over on that play. However, if the play is at first, the third baseman hustles back to cover third. He must do this in case the shortstop doesn't get over to cover and the runner going to second continues running and tries for third base.

Runners on First and Second

When a bunt is executed with runners on first and second, the force play at third base is a tough one to make. In order to get the runner, the bunt must be fielded immediately and thrown to the shortstop moving over to cover third base. If the third baseman has any doubt whatsoever, he should forget the force-out at third and go for the out at first base. Through experience, the third baseman and the catcher gain a good feel as to whether the play at third is possible.

With runners on first and second and less than two outs, the third baseman must be awake for several fielding possibilities. First of all, the runners may try a regular steal. Since the third baseman plays in, he must move back to third after every pitch to guard against this possibility. Another type of steal that may be attempted is the delayed steal. On the delayed steal, the runner waits until the catcher starts to throw the ball back to the pitcher and then takes off for third.

Another type of steal is called the fake bunt and steal. On this play, the hitter fakes the bunt and the runner or runners take off. The third baseman must rush the plate in case the hitter is actually bunting. This means the shortstop must cover third and tag the runner. It should be mentioned that anytime runners are on second or first and second, the third baseman has to be alert for any type of the steals mentioned.

When only second base is occupied with less than two out, a bunted ball should be played at first in most cases. It's very difficult for the third baseman to move in, pick up the bunt, and throw to the shortstop who, in turn, must tag the runner. Unless the ball is bunted hard and directly at the third baseman, he should take the sure out at first.

A BARE-HAND pickup is often a necessity at third base.

Double Plays

A third baseman in fast pitch has few chances to be involved in a double play because there simply aren't that many base runners normally. But when he does, a bad throw or misplay can be real trouble. When a ball is hit to the third baseman with a man on first only, he fires the ball to the second baseman. The throw should get to the second baseman just before he hits the bag. It should be slightly to the infield side of the base, not the outfield side.

With runners on first and second, there are a couple of options to be considered on the double play. If the ball is hit to the third baseman, he first touches third for the force-out. Where he goes for the next out depends on the speed of the runners. The surest out is usually first base, since a runner normally cannot go from home to first as fast as the runner goes from first to second. However, the runner on first may be very slow, while the hitter could be a left-hand batter and also very quick. These things should be considered prior to the pitch, not after the third baseman gets the ball.

Guarding the Foul Line

With nobody on base, and particularly with one or two outs, the third baseman plays back and close to the foul line. He is then able to stop hot liners from getting by him on his right. A hit that goes by the third baseman on his right side usually ends up as an extra-base hit.

When the third baseman plays back, he must always be alert for a drag bunt. A good drag bunter never gives his moves away and lays the bat out at the very last moment. A third baseman often must make a bare-hand pickup in order to make the play at first base in time.

THIRD BASE—SLOW PITCH

A third baseman in slow pitch is nearly a duplicate of the slow-pitch first baseman. He should be a good fielder with quick hands but doesn't have to be a speedy runner. A big, hard-hitting player with average speed and a strong arm will make a good third baseman.

Since he is faced with fielding hot liners and high bouncers and doesn't have to worry about bunts, the third baseman plays deep. His normal position is even with or several steps behind the bag. While most throws from third in fast pitch are made with a sidearm motion, the third baseman in slow pitch throws overhand because of the longer distance.

Because there are many hits and also many base runners in slow pitch, the third baseman will have many fielding and throwing opportunities. He should be particularly good at making throws to second base. Since the runner is not allowed to leave the base until the pitched ball reaches the plate, there is always a good chance for a force play at second.

MOST OUTFIELDERS prefer to catch the pop fly with hands extended over the head.

chapter 9
PLAYING THE OUTFIELD

It's common for an outfielder in fast pitch to go an entire game and make only one or two putouts. In some games he may not even handle the ball once. And then again he may have two tough chances in one inning. Because of this, the outfielder's most difficult task is staying alert.

Although the outfielder doesn't figure in the action nearly as much as the pitcher, catcher, and infielders, any mistake he makes is costly. When an infielder lets a ball get through him, it ordinarily means one extra base for the runner or runners. If an outfielder allows a ball to get past him, the runner usually manages to take at least two extra bases.

An outfielder doesn't have to be lightning fast or have a great throwing arm. But he should be able to throw quickly and accurately. Many times a player with average speed gets by very well in the outfield. When there is a choice to be made, the slower outfielders play either right or left field. The center fielder has more ground to cover and should have fairly good speed.

Because there are few outfield hits, a player who is an outstanding hitter but only an average fielder has a good chance of playing the outfield in fast pitch. Some of the finest hitters that played the outfield were neither fast nor had a great arm.

JUDGING THE FLY BALL

A beginning softball outfielder should spend as much time as possible working on catching fly balls. The more he has a chance to practice on catching pop flys and line drives, the faster he'll learn to judge the flight of the ball. Judging a fly ball is one of the skills that cannot be easily taught. Practice and hard work are the best teachers.

A very difficult play to judge is the low line drive that is hit directly at the fielder. This is primarily due to the fact it's hard to judge the speed of the ball. A fielder's natural instinct tells him to come in fast for the low liner. Although getting the jump on the ball is a big advantage in the outfield, you must be careful with the low line drive. This type of hit often starts low but continues to rise as it approaches the outfielder.

THE CATCH

How to catch the pop fly has been covered in the chapter on infielder play. However, the outfielder usually contends with higher and longer hit balls. Pop flys that are hit high enough for the outfielder to camp under are fairly easy to handle. Yet during a day game when there is a "high sky" (clear day and bright sun), an outfielder may be temporarily blinded and lose the ball. This can also happen at night when the outfielder looks directly into bright lights. Learning to shade your eyes and still not lose sight of the ball is all part of making the catch.

Inexperienced outfielders tend to panic when they lose sight of the ball for a moment and make useless moves. A good outfielder watches the ball from the time it comes off the bat until it's in the glove. If he loses it for a moment because of the sun, he does not give up. Instead, he keeps his eyes shaded until he again picks up the flight of the ball. Young outfielders may practice this play by intentionally looking away from a pop fly and then looking up again to see if they can still follow the ball.

All outfielders must learn to go back on long fly balls. When an outfielder sees that a ball is going to drive him back to make the catch, he must turn, run, and catch the ball over his shoulder. An outfielder goes after this type of fly ball in a similar way as an end in football catches a forward pass. He should never backpedal in trying to get back.

GROUND BALLS

Fielding ground balls properly in the outfield is just as important, or maybe more so, as catching the fly ball. In general, the outfield ground is not as smooth as the infield. Consequently, the need for getting in front of the ball and keeping the glove low is just as important to the outfielder as it is to the infielder.

Charging a ground ball and keeping your

MAKING THE CATCH in a bright sun is always difficult. An outfielder must shade his eyes to keep from losing sight of the ball.

OUTFIELDERS must charge ground ball with glove low to ground. Waiting for a ground ball may mean an extra base for the runner.

eye on it is the key to keeping a runner from taking an extra base. Because there are few hits in fast pitch, everytime a runner can gain an extra base it's a real bonus.

A fast runner can stretch a single into a double if the outfielder bobbles the ground ball or shows any slight hesitation as to where he is going to throw. Therefore, an outfielder should get rid of the ball as quickly as he can. He should always throw to the lead base and never throw behind the runner. Throwing behind the runner means throwing to the base the runner has already rounded.

A clever base runner will often round the base far enough to encourage the outfielder to throw behind him. At the instant the outfielder throws, the runner takes off for an extra base. It is very unusual to be able to trap the runner by throwing behind him. Play it safe whenever possible and throw to the lead base.

THE THROW

Where and how to throw the ball in from the outfield depends on several things. On a short single with nobody on base, the outfielder charges in on the ball. After fielding it, he throws it overhand on the fly to the fielder covering second. Whenever possible the throw from the outfield should be made with an overhand motion. Throwing overhand keeps the ball from curving, as it may happen when thrown sidearm.

In most cases, any throw made to home plate should bounce once before it reaches the catcher. The throw is handled much easier if it hits the ground about ten to fifteen feet in front of the plate. A catcher also has a better chance of making the tag if the throw is toward the third-base side of home plate.

When a hit gets past the outfielder, he must first run it down and then make an accurate throw to a relay man. Throwing accurately to the relay man is the most important part of the relay play. The throw should reach the relay man from waist to chest high on the fly. A throw that is too low or one that makes the infielder jump for the ball will cause a split-second delay. A fraction of a second may be all that is needed for the runner to score or take an extra base.

WHERE TO PLAY

Several things determine where the outfielders play. Among them are the number of outs, number of runners on base, the hitter, score of the game, type of field, and the inning.

In comparison to outfielders in baseball or slow pitch, fast-pitch outfielders play very shallow. This is because the pitchers in fast pitch are so overpowering that a good share of the balls hit to the outfield are pop flies and short singles. As a result, the center fielder plays even closer than both the other outfielders. A big part of his job is to catch the short pop flies hit behind the shortstop and second baseman.

When playing on an open field (a field without outfield fences) the outfielders must play a little deeper. Playing on an open field means that the outfielders must be especially careful to back up one another on any ball hit to the outfield.

At certain times the entire outfield may play either very deep or very shallow. For

OUTFIELDERS must back up one another on every play.

example, when there's a good long-ball hitter up with two outs and nobody on, the entire outfield can afford to play deep. On the other hand, if a runner on third represents the winning run and it's the bottom half of the last inning with less than two outs, the entire outfield plays extremely close. Any hit between the fielders or a long fly ball will end the game anyhow. When all the outfielders are in close, they have a chance to hold the runner on a short pop fly or even throw him out at the plate on a short hit. They also have a good chance of catching a low sinking line drive that would fall in for a hit if they were at the normal depth.

RIGHT FIELDER

In baseball much emphasis is placed on having a player with a strong arm play right field. This is based on the fact that the right fielder has to make the longest throw to third base. Because there are fewer base runners in fast pitch, a strong arm is not that important. It's much better to be able to get rid of the ball quickly and throw with accuracy.

Other than regular fielding responsibilities, the right fielder must always be alert and back up infield throws to first base. Due to the frequency of bunts in fast pitch, the right fielder's main job consists of backing up plays at first base. As soon as the right fielder sees a hitter square around to bunt, he moves in closer and toward the foul line, in case of an overthrow.

Since the center fielder is usually playing in a little closer then the other outfielders, the right fielder or left fielder (depending on where the ball is hit) should always back up the center fielder on any ball hit in that direction. Even when the center fielder is camped under an easy pop fly the right fielder should hustle over in case the center fielder loses the ball in the sun or bright lights.

Hit to Right

On a short hit to right field with nobody on, the right fielder charges the ball and quickly throws to second base. Don't worry about how far the runner rounds first; make the throw to second base and not to first. A single to right with first base occupied calls for the throw to be made to third base. Because this throw is fairly long, a one-bounce peg is a good idea rather than trying to throw the ball on the fly.

When a runner is on second, a hit to right field will usually score him. Unless the base runner represents the winning run in the late innings, throw the ball to second to keep the runner who got the hit from getting in scoring position. It's rare that a right fielder can get the runner at the plate unless he's pulled in very close.

The second baseman is the relay man on hits to right field. Any hard hit which gets past the right fielder usually means that a relay throw will be necessary. Although the outfielder must get the ball to the relay man without delay, the throw should not be made in haste.

Trying to throw the ball before getting a good grip often results in an error. This is an important consideration, especially on wet grass. During night games the grass is often damp, so grasping the ball firmly is a key factor in completing the throw. Throwing quickly and accurately to the relay man is much better than hurrying a hard throw that is difficult to handle.

As soon as the fielder has a firm grip on the ball, he should turn and look for the relay man. There is no time to look to see how the play is developing. Beginning and inexperienced players should practice often on improving their throws to the relay man.

CENTER FIELDER

A center fielder should be fast, capable of fielding ground balls well, and have a good, accurate arm. Because he plays a shallow outfield a good share of the time, he must also be able to go back well on long fly balls. He should be the most versatile player in the outfield.

Speed is a definite advantage for playing center field. However, the ability to get the jump on the ball is even more important. A fielder who has average to good speed, a good sense of judging fly balls and is able to get a quick start should make a fine center fielder.

In addition to backing up both of the other outfielders, the center fielder is responsible for backing up all throws made to second base. Backing up second is particularly important when a runner attempts to steal. Even good teams sometimes get mixed up on coverage at second. As a result, a catcher's throw may get through the infield untouched by either the second baseman or shortstop. If the center fielder is not backing up the play, the ball could go all the way to the outfield fence.

Hit to Center

The center fielder has the best view of the ball coming off the bat, so he can come in very fast on any short hits to center. Therefore, most throws he makes to either second or third base are on the fly. There are occasions when the center fielder may have to go into right center on an extra-base hit. In this case the throw to third may call for a one-bounce peg, just as it would if he were to throw to home.

All suggestions given for the right fielder for throwing to the relay man apply to the center fielder. The only exception is the relay man. On a ball hit to deep right center, the relay man is the second baseman. The shortstop will be the relay man on deep hits to center and left center field.

With a runner on second base, the center fielder usually has the best chance of any outfielder to throw out a runner at home on a short single to the outfield. Whether to throw to home or to second base is best learned through game experience. As we mentioned previously, the decision where to throw also depends on the situation and the runners involved.

LEFT FIELDER

Because a majority of hitters are right-handed, the left fielder usually has a little more action than the right fielder. Therefore he must be able to come in on a ground ball quickly and have good quick hands. Since he doesn't have to make the long throw to third, a fielder with an average arm may fit into the outfield well as a left fielder.

In addition to backing up the center fielder, the main responsibility of the left fielder is backing up third base. The shortstop is often moving to cover third on bunts and steals. And since this is one of the most difficult infield plays to execute properly, the chance of an overthrow is good.

When a runner is on second and a hitter squares to bunt, the left fielder moves in slightly. As soon as he sees where the bunt is picked up, he moves accordingly. For example, if the bunt is fielded on the third-base side of the pitcher's mound, he backs up the play more to the playing field side of the foul line. But if it's fielded on the first-

EVEN EXPERIENCED outfielders can lose the ball in the sun. Back-up man keeps runner from taking extra bases.

base side of the mound, he moves quickly into foul territory to back up the play.

Hit to Left

On most short hits to left field, the left fielder usually throws the ball on the fly to the infielders covering second or third base. On an extra-base hit, the relay man for the left fielder is the shortstop. However, since the left fielder plays closer to third base than other outfielders, it is sometimes better for the left fielder to make the throw to third himself rather than use the shortstop. On a play of this type the shortstop or the center fielder will usually shout instructions as to where the ball should be thrown.

GAME PREPARATION

During batting practice or just prior to the start of the game, outfielders should check the field carefully for bumps, bare spots in the grass, or any other unusual characteristics that may affect how they will play the ball. For example, during the course of a season, bare spots are worn in the grass where the outfielders stand. These spots are often bumpy, and ground balls may take bad hops when they hit this portion of the field. An alert outfielder will always try to charge a ground ball and make the pickup before it reaches these bare spots.

Check where the light poles are placed. In some instances a foul fly may be playable in an area where light poles or other structures such as dugouts, or even trees, are located. Running blindly into such an obstacle may not only change the result of the game, it could be the cause of a serious injury. Get a good feel for how far you can go before running into the outfield fence. Fields differ in design and often have varying distances to the individual outfield fences. Also, check the amount of room you have from the foul line to the bleachers or foul-line fences.

When playing on a strange field at night, look for low lights placed in your line of sight. Sometimes, lights from concession stands or other buildings may cause an outfielder to momentarily lose sight of low line drives. If the lights cannot be turned off or shaded, the outfielder must shade his eyes the best way he can.

Warm-up drills before the game can be very valuable for checking brightness and location of the sun in day games or poorly

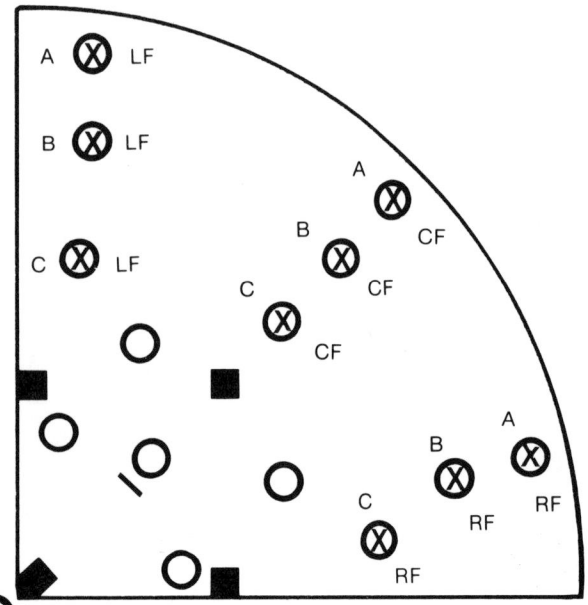

OUTFIELD PATTERNS—fast pitch. A—outfield deep. B—regular outfield depth. C—shallow outfield—used for cutting off winning run.

focused lights during night games. The warm-up drill can be extremely important in tournament games, when batting practice is not permitted. During the drill it's a good idea for the person hitting balls to the outfield to hit ground balls as well as fly balls. This gives the outfielders a better chance to check more field conditions, including the dampness of the grass.

OUTFIELD—SLOW PITCH

Having speedy outfielders in slow pitch is not only important, it is necessary for a team's success. There is no place for a slow-running outfielder with a poor arm in this game. A slow-pitch outfielder must do all the things required of a fast-pitch outfielder. Furthermore, he must do all these things more often.

Slow-pitch teams have the choice of playing their outfield in two basic patterns. First they may play with a short-center fielder and three deep outfielders. In this pattern, the short fielder is responsible for short pop flies and line drives hit up the middle. He may even throw out a runner on second when a hard ground ball is hit directly at him.

A short fielder should be a player with both the strong points of an infielder and outfielder. In addition to the responsibilities mentioned, the short fielder backs up second base and often becomes the relay man on extra-base hits.

The second outfield pattern consists of four deep outfielders. Currently, this appears to be the more common way of playing the outfield in slow pitch. Playing four deep outfielders cuts down on long extra-base hits. However, it is not without disadvantages. Low line drives and short pop flies can drop for hits that could be caught by a short fielder. Nevertheless, as slow-pitch hitters improved over the years, long, hard line drives have become the rule, not the exception. As a result, playing four deep outfielders is the better way of reducing the number of total base hits.

Most of the previous instructional material offered for fast-pitch outfielders also applies to slow pitch. This includes all portions on throwing, fielding, and backing up other outfielders and infielders. However, slow-pitch outfielders are not concerned with backing up bases on bunts or steals. Also, they always play deeper than the fast-pitch outfielders.

OUTFIELD PATTERNS—slow pitch. ●—three deep outfielders, one short fielder. X—four deep outfielders.

BEGINNERS HAVE much better control if they use a choke grip. Many outstanding fast-pitch hitters use the choke grip.

chapter 10
HITTING AND RUNNING

Many well-respected baseball and softball players sincerely believe that great hitters are born and not made. To some degree this is probably true, since hitting requires good eyesight, coordination, and quick reactions. Nevertheless, a poor hitter who receives proper instruction, practices often, and has a sincere desire to improve can become a good hitter.

Although there are basic fundamentals that should be followed, any player who consistently makes contact with the ball is doing something right. Too often, inexperienced and well-meaning parents offer young players suggestions that are not really helpful. In some cases they do more harm than good.

When a young player or an experienced hitter fails to make contact consistently, then it's time for a good batting coach to give him help. Sometimes the problem is very minor and one small tip may correct the problem. On the other hand, the problem may be due to a bad habit developed over a long period of time. It will probably take a little longer to correct a difficulty of this type. In some cases it could even be a physical defect. For example, the player may have poor eyesight and simply need glasses. Even an injury may contribute to a change in the player's batting average. This is a possibility that often is overlooked. It's quite common for an injured player to unknowingly favor an injury which, in turn, changes his normal swing or stance.

FAST PITCH IS DIFFERENT

Hitting in fast pitch is much different than hitting in baseball. First of all, the pitcher is closer and the ball gets to the plate quicker than it does in baseball. Secondly, a softball breaks more then a baseball, due to the fact that the softball is larger and has greater surface area.

It has been proven time and time again that a fine baseball hitter is not able to hit a great softball pitcher. By the same token, a good fast-pitch hitter has trouble hitting in slow pitch. The primary reason for this is timing. If a good baseball hitter quits playing baseball and concentrates on fast pitch, he will adjust his timing and eventually become a good hitter in fast pitch. Although there are exceptions to every rule, it's rare that a player can play both games in the same season and hit well in both sports.

Some parents will not permit their sons to play softball because they believe it will be harmful to a possible future career in baseball. This is really not very logical since some of the finest hitters in the major leagues were once softball players. And some players have come out of baseball and turned into fine fast-pitch hitters.

THE BEGINNER

Unless the young hitter is unusually strong, he should "choke up" (move his hands up toward the large end) on the bat. Choking up will give him much better control. Many of the good hitters in fast pitch choke up on every pitch. Some take a longer grip on the first two strikes and then shorten the grip to gain better control.

The beginner should be encouraged to feel comfortable with the bat he chooses and not worry about the model. It's true that using a heavy bat will give you a little more distance, but there's no advantage if you can't bring it around in time.

Besides weight, the length is another point to consider when selecting a bat. If the young player is responsible for furnishing his own bat, he should have a chance to swing it before purchasing it. A bat that is too long can give a youngster as much trouble as one that is too heavy. In most cases, the length of the bat is stamped on the end of the handle.

STANCE

There is probably too much emphasis placed on the importance of the stance. A good hitter can hit the ball in almost any stance, and a poor hitter has trouble regardless of where and how he stands. One of the better hitters in major softball not only took a completely unorthodox stance, he shuffled his feet on every pitch. Nevertheless, finding a comfortable stance is the first step in learning to hit.

MEDIUM GRIP. Most hitters use a medium grip.

LONG GRIP. Long-ball hitters with strong wrists prefer the long grip.

Just as in baseball, three basic stances are used in softball.

Open stance: In an open stance, the front foot is placed farther from the plate than the rear foot. This stance is often used by the pull hitter.

Closed stance: In a closed stance, the front foot is placed closer to the plate. An opposite field hitter normally uses this type of stance.

Square stance: In a square stance, both feet are the same distance from the plate.

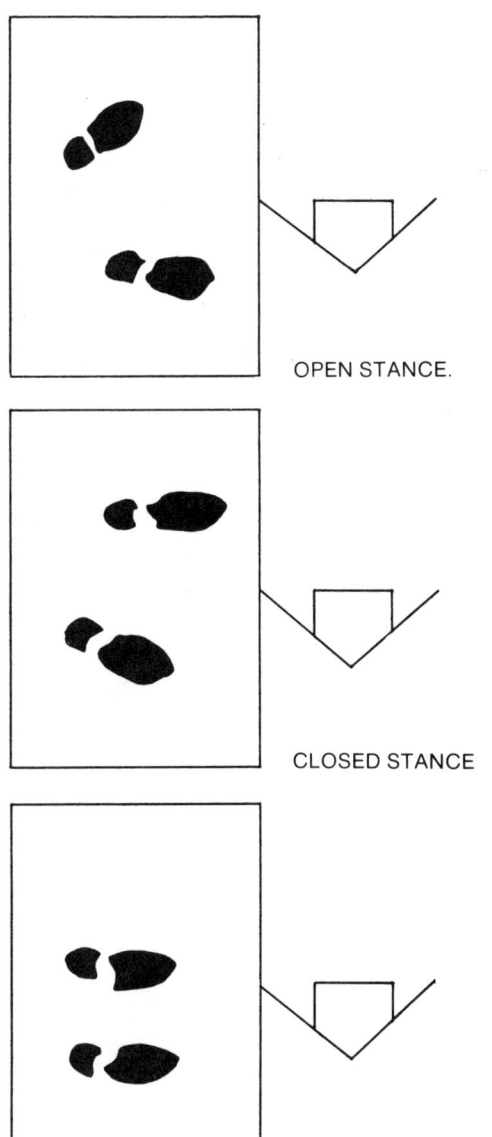

OPEN STANCE.

CLOSED STANCE

SQUARE STANCE.

Most hitters use the square stance. The legs are spread apart about 12 to 18 inches, with the feet pointing directly toward the plate.

Regardless of where the feet are placed, there are several things that apply to every batting stance. As the hitter gets set for the pitch, he takes a nearly erect position. His weight should be evenly distributed on the balls of the feet, with knees slightly bent.

A majority of the hitters hold the bat at approximately the same angle. The angle at which the bat is held is of little importance unless it has an adverse effect on the swing. Hips and shoulders are level, and the arms—with elbows bent—are held away from the body.

Particularly in fast pitch, the elbow of the rear arm is held shoulder high. In this way, the hitter can get up on the rise ball more consistently. Once the hitter starts dropping the rear elbow down, he's going to have trouble with the rise.

GETTING READY

Being ready to hit is just as important as any other part of hitting. You can't go up to the plate thinking about anything else but hitting the ball. In other words, there must be complete concentration on the contest between the hitter and the pitcher. Any other action on the field or in the stands should be locked out of your mind.

While you're in the dugout, watch every move the pitcher makes until you get a feel for his throwing rhythm. This is an excellent time to see if there is anything he does that tips his pitches. Things to look for on tipping pitches are discussed in the chapter on the "complete pitcher." When you're in the "on-deck circle," get set and swing the bat in time with the pitcher's delivery as he throws to the hitter.

If you notice that a pitcher likes to throw quickly, with little time used between pitches, take your time getting from the on-deck circle into the batter's box. However, if he likes to take his time, hustle to the batter's box. In other words, break his rhythm.

When you are walking from the on-deck circle to the batter's box look at your third-base coach. This may be a good time to look for a signal, rather than after you get set in the box. Looking for a signal after you have set yourself sometimes breaks your concentration. It also gives the opposing team a better chance to pick up the coach's signal.

IN THE BOX

Once you're in the batter's box and your stance feels comfortable, get the bat in a ready position. Some batters have a habit of swinging the bat back and forth as they wait for the pitch. All that swinging does nothing except waste time, and often the hitter is not ready when the pitcher releases the ball.

Young hitters are often told to keep their swing level. If the ball comes in right down the middle, belt high; then the swing is reasonably level. But there is no way in the world you can hit a drop ball, knee high,

AT POINT OF contact, full power is achieved. The front leg is straight and the rear leg is slightly bent.

with a level swing. In order to hit a drop well, the swing is very similar to hitting a golf ball. To hit a high rise ball you have to get "on top" of it; in fact, it is almost a downward swing.

Practically every young player wants to hit with power, and of course he feels the harder he swings the farther the ball goes. A young player who continually swings hard often develops an underswing. A player with an underswing will normally have trouble hitting the rise ball consistently. Usually, overswinging is accompanied by a long stride, which further aggravates the problem of trying to hit the rise.

STRIDE

When a ball player is said to have a picture swing, it really means he has a smoothly coordinated stride and swing. For fast pitch, a short stride of about six to eight inches is best. The foot is slid forward just slightly above the ground. It's very important that the forward stride is timed with the pitcher's delivery. Striding too early or too late usually affects the actual swing. For example, an over-anxious hitter normally hurries the stride. He either swings ahead of the ball or simply misses it trying to adjust his timing. Hitters who stride too early can sometimes delay the stride by twisting the front hip in toward the plate just prior to the stride. This slight twist will delay the stride enough yet still allow the arms to be in proper hitting position.

Always keep the forward stride straight ahead. Young hitters should work hard on this phase of hitting. If the youngster gets in the habit of stepping away from the plate, he will find it very difficult to change later on.

ON THE PITCH

As the pitcher delivers, the stride begins with wrists cocked. Keeping the wrists cocked allows the hitter to hit any type of

WEIGHT IS transferred from rear foot to front foot as swing is completed.

WRISTS ROLL over on smooth follow-through.

pitch. Once you drop those wrists down, you have lessened your chances of making good contact.

As you complete the swing, the cocked wrists and bent arms end up with the arms fully extended. At the time of contact, full power of the swing is achieved. Also, the weight that was formerly on the rear foot is transferred to the front foot.

When contact is made, the front leg is straight and the rear leg is bent. If a hitter is consistently popping up, check for a bent front leg and a long stride. Obviously, this isn't the only reason he may be hitting under the ball, but it's one fault that *can* be easily detected.

At the end of the swing the wrists roll over as the follow-through is completed. If all the portions of the swing are correct, the follow-through will take care of itself.

HIT IT WHERE IT'S PITCHED

One batting fundamental taught by all coaches—whether it's baseball, fast pitch or slow pitch—is to hit the ball where it's pitched. In other words, if the ball is pitched inside, the ball should be met in front of the plate and pulled to left field; right field if you're left-handed. When it's pitched across the heart of the plate, the ball is hit with the bat straight across the plate and is driven to center field. If the ball is pitched to the outside of the plate, the contact should be made at the back of the plate. A right-handed hitter should hit the outside pitch to right, and the left-hand hits the outside pitch to left field.

Batting tips for hitting the ball where it's pitched seem logical and sound good. However, to do it properly is another thing.

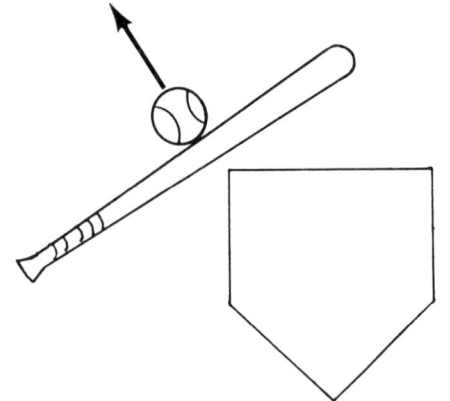

MEET THE inside pitch out in front of the plate.

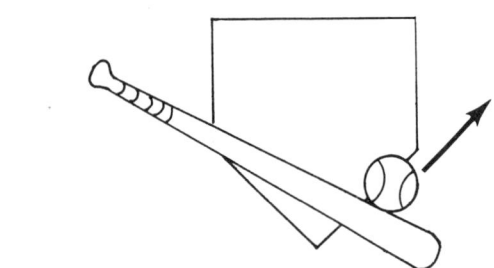

THE OUTSIDE pitch is met at the back of the plate.

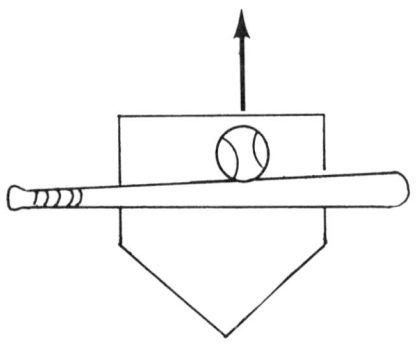

A PITCH over the center of the plate is hit up the center of the diamond.

HIT THE BALL WHERE IT'S PITCHED.

When facing a top-notch pitcher in fast pitch, you're lucky to get the bat on the ball—let alone hit it where it's pitched. Nevertheless, if a pitcher continually pitches you outside, and you persist in trying to pull the pitch, you're not likely to hit the ball solid. When hitters try to pull outside pitches, they either miss the ball completely or often hit the ball at the end of the bat. This normally results in pop flies and weakly hit ground balls.

Hitters who continually fail to meet the inside pitch out in front of the plate will usually hit the ball on the handle. Many times a hitter will try to correct this problem by moving farther away from the plate. Although moving away from the plate may help a little, it won't solve the problem entirely. In fact it may cause him to have difficulty with outside pitches.

RAISING YOUR BATTING AVERAGE

We said earlier in the chapter that some players are just better hitters than others because of their physical makeup. But whether you have natural ability or not, there are certain basic facts regarding hitting that cannot be overlooked. For example, if you want to be able to maintain a good batting average against good pitchers, then you have to face good pitchers often. An inexperienced hitter who has trouble hitting a rise ball will have a much better chance of improving by facing a good rise-ball pitcher frequently.

Hitting is like any other part of the game: To do it well, you must do it often. A young player can receive the finest instructions from a great hitter on grip, stance, stride, and swing; but if he doesn't practice long and often, results will be slow in coming.

In addition to routine practice, there must be a steady progression in the type of competition the player faces. In some cases, youngsters may face only average pitching for one or even two seasons in a row. When they come up against an outstanding pitcher, they are likely to be almost helpless at the plate. Their inability to hit at this time has nothing to do with basic technique. It's simply due to the fact they are not used to good pitching. In this situation, a coach or manager should be very careful not to make any drastic changes in basic stances or swings. After the youngsters face better pitchers, they will start meeting the ball more often.

OUT OF A SLUMP

At some time or another, even the best hitters get into a batting slump. Why a hitter gets into a slump—or gets out of it, for that matter—is sometimes very hard to explain. Rather than get into a long discussion of all the mental factors and batting techniques involved, we'll stick to two common problems.

First, let's assume that a hitter is having trouble hitting the rise ball. Rather than trying to study every possible reason, schedule extra batting practice for the hitter and use a pitcher who throws a good rise.

Start by having the pitcher throw at half speed, without throwing stuff. This allows the hitter to adjust his timing and get loosened up. After a few minutes, the pitcher can begin throwing the rise ball at about three-quarters speed. On the first few pitches, get the batter to actually swing above the rise. This exercise starts him thinking about getting on top of the pitch. At this point the hitter can then begin to take his normal cut.

After the batter hits several good "solid" shots at the three-quarter speed, have the pitcher throw a few rise balls at full speed. To complete the practice, the pitcher can mix his pitches for a few minutes. If possible, repeat the routine several days in a row. By using a practical approach of this type, the hitter normally will start moving the rise ball more consistently.

Another pitch that hitters commonly have trouble with is the drop. Once again, the batting practice approach we discussed for the rise should work well for the drop. Use the same steps in the practice routine. However, instead of swinging over the ball on the first few three-quarter speed drops, get the bat down under the ball.

Good batting coaches are hard to find, but a good one can often correct a hitter's fault after watching him for a few swings during a game. If you are having trouble, it's far better to ask the advice of someone who knows what he's talking about rather than experiment with changes yourself. Also, guard against receiving too much advice from the other teammates, who wish to help but usually confuse you more than they help.

BUNTING

A well-placed bunt in fast pitch can be as important as an extra-base hit. However, beginners should work on getting the bunt down properly before trying to place it in any particular spot.

As in baseball, there are two types of bunts used in fast pitch: the sacrifice bunt and the bunt for a hit (often called a drag bunt). The sacrifice bunt means that the runner is giving himself up by clearly showing the opposition he is going to bunt.

The main aim of the bunter is to move the runner to the next base. On a sacrifice bunt, the hitter should not worry about getting out of the box fast. Every possible effort should be made to get the ball down fair without popping it up.

When the hitter is sacrificing, it's best to stand toward the front of the batter's box since it gives him a better chance to get the bunt down fair. As the pitcher begins his delivery, the rear foot is usually brought forward and even with the front one. Feet are spread from 12 to 18 inches. However, if the hitter feels more comfortable stand-

94 HITTING AND RUNNING

ON A SACRIFICE bunt, the hitter faces the pitcher with hands well spread on the bat. Ball contact is made on lower half of bat circumference.

ing very close to the plate, the front foot is moved backward and placed even with the rear foot. In either case the hitter should be facing the pitcher with hands well spread on the bat. The bat is held parallel to the ground, with the lower hand in the normal spot near the handle and the other hand at about the trademark.

When taking the bunting position, never move the bottom hand. Always slide the top hand up to a spot near the trademark. Knees and hips should be slightly bent, with your weight on the balls of your feet.

There is no set way to hold the bat with the top hand. Most players let the bat rest loosely on the tips of the fingers, with the thumb gripping the top part of the bat. As the ball approaches the hitter, the bat is held still—as if the hitter were going to catch the ball on the bat. Actual contact with the pitch should be made so that the ball strikes the lower half of the bat. Thus the ball is hit toward the ground. If the ball hits the top half of the bat it will be popped up and an easy double play may result.

Placing the sacrifice bunt in fast pitch is not easy, but it can be done by adjusting the position of the bat. A right-hand bunter wishing to bunt toward the third-base side, places the bat at an angle similar to that of a pull hitter as he makes contact on a regular swing. On a bunt to first, the angle of the bat is similar to that of an opposite field hitter's swing. In fast pitch, it is usually best to bunt the ball toward the pitcher, since the first and third basemen play very close on the sacrifice bunt. When bunting toward the pitcher, the bat is placed straight across the plate.

In a bunt situation, most pitchers prefer to throw the rise ball. Therefore, the bunter must be very alert and keep the bat above the path of the ball. Even experienced players occasionally pop up the bunt because they fail to concentrate on letting the ball hit the lower portion of the bat.

DRAG BUNT

In order for the drag bunt to work properly, it should be a surprise to the defensive infielders. Therefore, the hitter must begin his normal stride and swing, but at the last

DRAG BUNT. Hitter begins with normal hitting stride. At the last moment, the top hand is slid up on the bat . . .

HITTING AND RUNNING

THE HITTER is actually bunting and running at the same time. Ball contact is made on lower half of bat...

THE BUNT and stride is one continuous motion as the batter breaks for first.

moment he slides his top hand up on the bat. The top hand is moved up while the ball is on its way. Most good drag bunters move the top hand up about six to eight inches rather than up to the trademark as in a sacrifice bunt.

Part of the effectiveness of the drag bunt is due to the jump the hitter gets toward first. Since the batter takes his normal stride he makes contact with the ball on his front foot. This stride is one continuous motion as the batter breaks for first. In other words, the hitter is really bunting and running at the same time.

A hitter who has a reputation for being a good bunter has an added advantage. Infielders must play him close at all times, so he often gets ground ball hits through the infield that would ordinarily be outs. A speedy left-hand hitter who bunts well makes an excellent leadoff man.

RUNNING THE BASES

Getting a quick start is the most important part of good base running. Although natural speed is a big help, it must be used properly. For example, taking too wide a turn can cost the runner valuable seconds no matter how fast he is.

On a hit to right or right center field, the hitter has a fairly good view of the ball. In most instances, he can judge himself whether or not he can take an extra base. Nevertheless, he should keep his eyes and ears open for help from the first-base

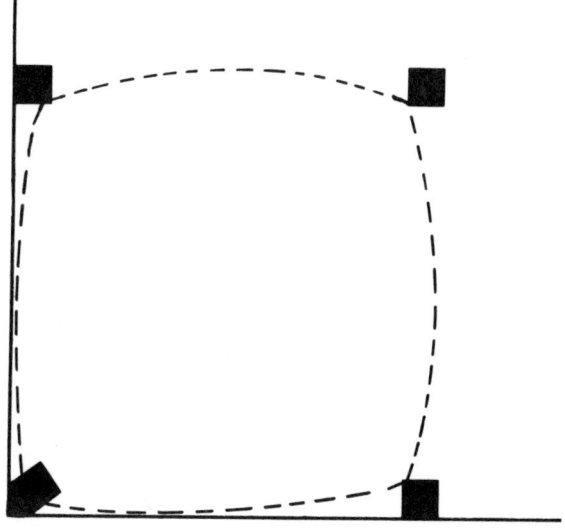

RUNNERS MAKE a sharp turn and hit the inside of the base with right foot. Too wide a turn costs valuable time.

coach. On a hit to left field, the runner must look for a signal from the first-base coach. Turning to look where the ball is will cost the runner time or may even cause him to miss first base.

When a hitter sees the ball going into the outfield, on the ground or in the air, he should run about two to three feet outside the foul line. As he nears the bag, the hitter adjusts his stride so he can make a sharp turn and touch the inside corner of the bag with his right foot. If the hit appears to be just a single he rounds the bag, stops, and quickly checks to see if the fielder has possession of the ball. The runner always must be alert in case the outfielder bobbles the ball or makes a poor throw to the lead base. Never turn your back on the play.

On an extra-base hit, the runner must make a snap decision on his way to second base. He has to decide whether he will slide, stand up, or round second base. If the extra-base hit goes to right field, the runner should look at the third-base coach for help. Ordinarily, the runner can make up his own mind what to do on an extra-base hit to left or center field. On the way to second or third, the runner should run slightly to the outfield side of the base path. Thus he can always make a sharp turn as he touches the inside of the bag with his right foot. Anytime a runner is going from second to third, he must look at the third-base coach for help.

STEALING

Getting a quick start and learning to anticipate the pitcher's release of the ball are the two things necessary to be a good base stealer. Since a runner cannot leave a base until the pitcher releases the ball, anticipating the release is more important than speed. Regardless of how fast a runner is, if he waits until he sees the ball leave the pitcher's hand and then breaks, he is not likely to steal many bases. The break from the base must be made so that the runner is on the move at the exact moment the ball leaves the pitcher's hand.

SLIDING

Learning to slide properly is important for two reasons. First, it gives the runner a much better chance of being safe on a tag

TO STEAL successfully, runner must anticipate release of ball from the pitcher's hand.

DEMONSTRATION OF start of straight-in slide. Practice sliding on grass, but remove spikes to prevent possible injury.

END OF straight-in slide.

play. And second, a proper slide will prevent possible serious injuries.

The hook, or fall-away, slide and the straight-in slide are the types of slides most commonly used. Another type of slide, the head-first slide, is not recommended for the beginner.

One key factor in making a good slide is to give yourself ample time to execute the move. In other words, you must make up your mind that you are going to slide several strides ahead of the base. A last minute slide is usually ineffective and frequently ends up with the runner or fielder being hurt.

A runner faced with the possibility of sliding at second must make up his own mind. When going into third the runner will be guided by the third-base coach. The runner trying to score at home plate may or may not have help. It's the responsibility of the on-deck hitter to advise the runner as to whether or not to slide.

On a straight or direct slide, the top leg is kept nearly straight while the bottom leg is bent at the knee. As contact is made with the bag, the bottom leg is drawn up. This gives the runner a chance to quickly rise.

A hook, or fall-away, slide is used to avoid the reaching infielder's tag. When an infielder takes the throw on the inside of the base, the runner falls away to the outside of the base and vice versa. A hook slide is executed by hurling the body away from the infielder and then hooking the bag with the right toe, if the slide is made to the left of the base. Reverse the procedure if the slide is to be made to the right side of the bag.

98 HITTING AND RUNNING

START OF hook slide to outside corner of bag. Hook slide is executed by hurling body away from base and hooking inside corner of bag with instep.

END OF HOOK slide to outside corner of bag.

HITTING AND RUNNING 99

START OF hook slide to inside corner of bag.

END OF HOOK slide to inside corner of bag.

THE HEAD-FIRST slide is not recommended for the beginner.

HITTING AND RUNNING—SLOW PITCH

Practically all of the information covered on running the bases and how to slide in the fast-pitch section is directly applicable to slow pitch. Therefore, we will not repeat that material in the slow-pitch section.

Like any other technique in softball, hitting slow pitch requires practice before any success can be realized. Nearly anyone who has played any type of baseball or fast-pitch softball can hit a ball that is lobbed into them. But hitting consistently for base hits is not so easy.

It's very interesting to watch a former baseball or fast-pitch player try to hit slow pitch for the first time. He usually violates all the fundamentals he learned in his former specialty. Swinging too hard and taking his eyes off the ball are common mistakes made.

By applying the same basic fundamentals learned in fast pitch or baseball, the inexperienced slow-pitch hitter will get his share of base hits. Of course, the first requirement is to play the game often. Otherwise he will not be able to properly adjust his timing, and he will soon become discouraged.

Even though the ball comes down at the

batter in slow pitch, the stride, wrist action, and swing must all be coordinated just as in baseball or fast pitch. If a ball passes over the plate shoulder high, the hitter still must get up on top of the pitch. When it comes in knee high, the golf-type swing with good wrist action is needed.

Hitting the ball where it's pitched applies just as much in slow pitch as it does in baseball and fast pitch. A good place hitter can maintain a very high batting average in this game. Slow pitch also offers a chance for the strong long-ball hitter to enjoy a long career. There are positions such as third, first, and catcher that do not require great running speed. Therefore, the strong long-ball hitter with only average or slow speed can play the game for many years.

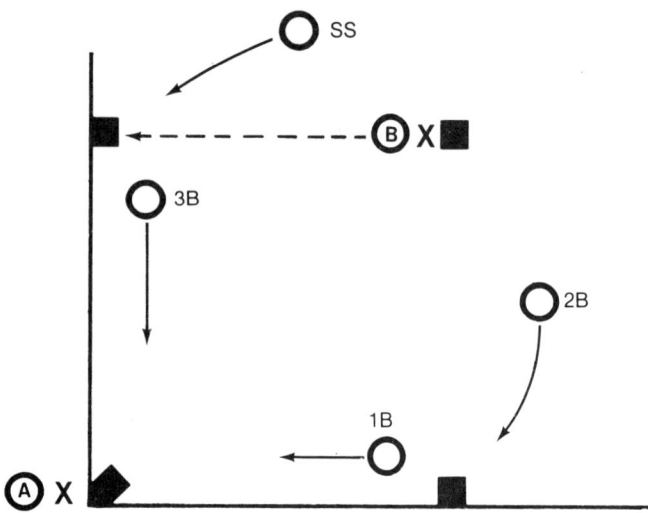

FAKE BUNT AND STEAL. Hitter (A) fakes bunt, runner (B) steals third. Shortstop must try to cover third on the play.

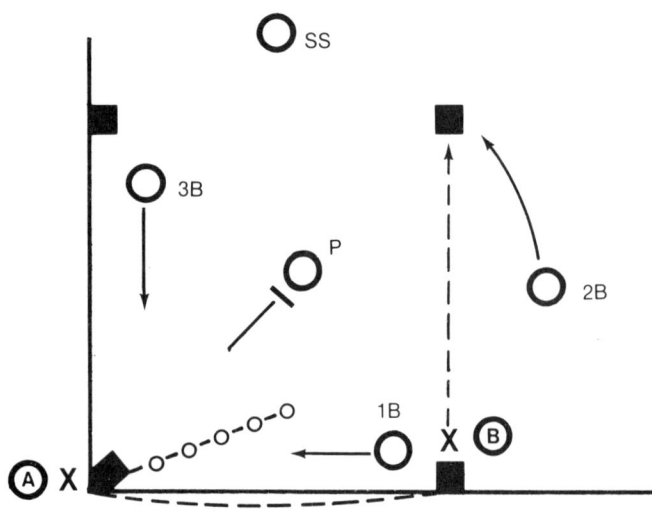

STEAL AND BUNT. Runner (B) steals with right-hand hitter at bat. Second baseman moves to cover second base. Hitter (A) bunts toward first base. First base is left uncovered. Play can be used with man on first and second also.

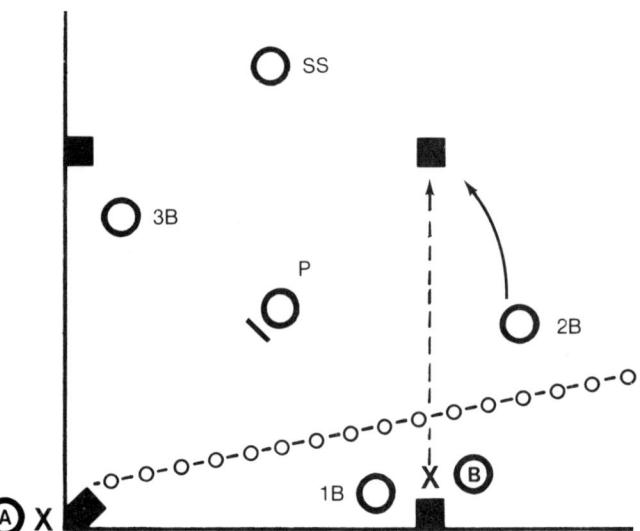

HIT AND RUN. Runner B steals. Second baseman moves to cover second. Hitter A hits ball through hole left by second baseman.

chapter 11
OFFENSIVE STRATEGY

All great softball teams have outstanding pitching, fielding, and hitting. When two great teams play each other, it's often said that breaks decide the winner. It's also said that winners make their own breaks. And one of the best ways to make your own breaks is by using good sound strategy.

Bunting certainly figures into game strategy a great deal. However, one of the most overrated plays in softball is to bunt with a runner on first and nobody out. If more teams would keep accurate statistics, they would find this is not always a good percentage move.

There are several things to consider before the bunt is used with a runner on first. Number one concern should be the hitter. Is he a good bunter? Number two concern is the runner. Is he fast and is he a good base runner? Another important concern is the hitter or hitters who follow the player who bunts. Are the two hitters who follow the bunter high percentage hitters? If the answer to any one of these questions is "no," your chances of scoring by hitting away or some other move are about the same as sacrificing.

Keep in mind that when a team uses the sacrifice bunt, it gives up one man to advance another. In other words by sacrificing, a team willingly gives up 33 1/3 percent of their offensive opportunity just to advance a runner into better scoring position. But what are the chances of scoring if the sacrifice is not successful? For example, a good fast-pitch team will frequently throw the runner out at second base. In some cases, the sacrifice is popped up and turned into an easy out, or even a double play. All of these factors must be considered by coaches and managers as to whether this play is advantageous under given circumstances.

Most supporters of bunting with a man on first base contend that anytime a team bunts, there is a good possibility that the defense will make an error. To a very small degree this is true, but a good fast-pitch infield handles the bunt as well as a ground ball play. However, if a team has a weak member in the infield—especially at first, second, or third—the bunt becomes a much better percentage play.

The previous discussion is not intended to completely discourage bunting with a runner on first. But it is intended to encourage managers and coaches to consider all the facts. Indeed, there are advantages of using the sacrifice bunt in this situation. Once a runner reaches second, the opportunities for scoring are increased considerably.

What are the alternatives to sacrificing with a runner on first? First, a team may leave the runner on first regardless of his speed. An infield single or a play at first will still advance him to second. An extra-base hit to the outfield may advance the runner to third or even score him. Of course there are disadvantages, too, such as the hitter popping up or hitting into a double play.

Another alternative consists of inserting a speedy runner at first. This move gives you the possibility of the runner scoring on a long single or double. It also gives the team an option to steal second base. If the steal is successful, the chances of scoring are increased a great deal. However, if the steal is unsuccessful, a team has not only lost a base runner but also 33 1/3 percent of its offensive potential in that inning.

With runners on first and second and nobody out, the sacrifice presents a better scoring opportunity than with a runner on first only. If the sacrifice is successful two runners are in scoring position. The runner on third has almost unlimited possibilities of scoring.

Probably the finest spot for the sacrifice occurs when a runner is on second with nobody out. In this case, the runner has all the advantages. First of all, he can get an excellent jump toward third. It is almost impossible to get the runner, since the play is not a force-out and requires a tag. And even if the batter pops up, the runner can get back to second with little chance of being doubled up. This is due to the fact that the second baseman will be covering first and the shortstop is covering third base.

FAKE BUNT AND STEAL

When runners are on second or first and second, a fake bunt and steal is often an excellent play to use. The fake bunt by the hitter is the key to a successful steal. As soon as the hitter squares to bunt, the first and third basemen charge. This means that the shortstop must run to cover third, a difficult play to make anytime. One thing that the batter must be careful to do is square around at the last possible moment. If he squares too soon, it gives the shortstop more time to get started toward third base.

STEAL AND BUNT

One of the plays rarely used in fast pitch is a play called steal and bunt. It calls for a very specific situation. The best time to use this play is with a runner on first, one or two outs, and a right-hand hitter at the plate. Normally, the defense is not expecting the bunt, and with a right-hander at the plate the second baseman covers second on the steal. This play is started by the runner breaking for second as soon as the ball leaves the pitcher's hand. Usually, the second baseman then moves to cover second on the steal. At this point, the hitter drops the bunt—which means the first and third baseman charge. If the play works as expected, there will be nobody covering first base. Runners are now at first and second without the loss of an out.

DOUBLE STEAL

Although we have already discussed using the double steal with a man on first and second and faking a bunt, the double steal also may be tried with a runner on first and third. This play is started by the runner on first stealing second. If the catcher decides to throw to second base, the runner on third breaks for the plate. The runner on third must watch carefully to see if the shortstop moves in close to cut the throw off and trap the runner as he breaks for the plate.

HIT AND RUN

Although this play is used often in baseball it's not very effective in fast pitch. The main reason it is seldom used is due to the difficulty in trying to place the hit behind the runner.

As the ball leaves the pitcher's hands, the runner on first breaks for second. With a right-hand hitter at the plate, the second baseman moves to cover second base. The hitter must swing late and try to hit the ball in the hole left by the second baseman. Even if the second baseman recovers in time to field the ball, he is not likely to make the play at second base. As a result, the double play cannot be made and the move is as good as a sacrifice bunt. However, if the ball gets through the hole, the runner can usually make it to third base since he has a good jump to begin with.

SIGNALS

Strategy depends on all players to execute their part properly. Proper execution relies heavily on the player's ability to read signals that coaches use for starting various plays. If either the runner or hitter misses a signal, strategy may backfire and turn into a disadvantage. Therefore, coaches *must* impress upon young players the importance of always watching signals.

Signals should be arranged so they are not easily picked up by the opposing team. Yet they should not be so complicated that they confuse the hitters and runners. Most coaches use a "key" sign which means that a play is on. Another signal will follow that tells the player what specific play is to be used.

ONE LAST WORD

As in any sport, a player gets out of softball exactly what he puts into it. Anyone willing to learn and work hard will always have an excellent chance of achieving success.

Along that road to success, the softball player must develop a desire to win. However, coaches and managers who preach winning at any cost can warp a young player's attitude. Youngsters who play under constant pressure to win at any cost often become frustrated and confused individuals if they are not winning every game every day they play.

One important piece of advice to remember is to never, never give up on yourself. One or two bad games—or even a bad season—is no reason to throw away a career by giving up. Even after embarrassing and humbling defeats, a win over a tough opponent will always wash away the sour grapes of a loss.

appendix: league and tournament scheduling

One of the most important functions and responsibilities of the League or Tournament Director is the game schedule.

Scheduling games by using the proper method and recognized scheduling procedures will result in less problems for the Organizing Committee as well as make the competition interesting and fair.

There are a number of different methods for scheduling League and Tournament contests; however, the round robin for Leagues and double-elimination for tournaments seem to be the most commonly used.

The double-elimination tournament requires a much longer period of play than the single-elimination. Each team must be defeated twice before being eliminated from further competition.

Requiring an even longer period of time for completion is the round-robin tournament. However, the round-robin provides more participation than any other type of tourney. Every team competes against every other team, which stimulates interest throughout the tournament.

The final outcome in round-robin is decided on a percentage basis. The winner is determined according to the percentage of victories, which is obtained by dividing the number of victories by the number of games played.

The single-elimination tournament is the quickest method of determining a winner. However, it has a disadvantage of providing fewer opportunities for teams to play.

Aside from the regular elimination tourney, a consolation tournament may be conducted with losers from the first round of play participating. This arrangement enables every entry to play in at least two games.

On the following pages some round-robin and double-elimination schedules and brackets are shown.

HOW TO MAKE A LEAGUE SCHEDULE

Key-schedules for a round robin are shown below. In order to make use of them, teams draw or are assigned numbers. Then pick the proper schedule—5, 6, 7, 8, 10, or 12 teams. Leagues of 9 or 11 teams use the next higher schedule with a "bye" for the teams scheduled to play a number for which there is no corresponding club.

5 Teams			10 Teams			
1—2	3—1	3—4	1—2	4—10	10—12	6—7
3—4	4—6	5—6	3—4	6—9		4—11
		7—8	5—6		1—4	
	7 Teams		7—8	1—8	2—6	1—9
2—3	1—2	2—3	9—10	2—9	3—5	2—10
5—1	3—4	4—5		3—6	7—10	3—11
	5—6	6—7		4—7	8—12	4—12
3—5		8—1	1—3	5—10	9—11	5—7
4—2	1—3		2—4			6—8
	2—4	3—5	5—9	1—9	1—5	
4—5	5—7	2—6	6—8	2—10	2—4	1—10
3—1		4—8	7—10	3—7	3—6	2—11
	1—4	7—1		4—6	7—11	3—12
5—2	2—6		1—4	5—8	8—10	4—7
1—4	3—7		2—6		9—12	5—8
		4—6	3—9	1—10		6—9
6 Teams	1—5	7—3	5—7	2—5	1—6	
1—2	2—3	8—2	8—10	3—8	2—3	1—11
3—4	6—7	1—5		4—9	4—5	2—12
5—6			1—5	6—7	7—12	3—7
	1—6	5—7	2—3		8—9	4—8
2—3	2—5	8—3	4—8	12 Teams	10—11	5—9
4—5	4—7	6—1	6—10	1—2		6—10
6—1		2—4	7—9	3—4	1—7	
	1—7			5—6	2—8	1—12
3—6	3—5	5—8	1—6	7—8	3—9	2—7
4—2	4—6	6—3	2—7	9—10	4—10	3—8
5—1		2—7	3—10	11—12	5—11	4—9
	2—7	4—1	4—5		6—12	5—10
6—2	3—6		8—9	1—3		6—11
5—3	4—5	1—3		2—5	1—8	
4—1		2—5	1—7	4—6	2—9	
	8 Teams	4—7	2—8	7—9	3—10	
5—2	1—2	6—8	3—5	8—11	5—12	

Double Elimination—8 Teams

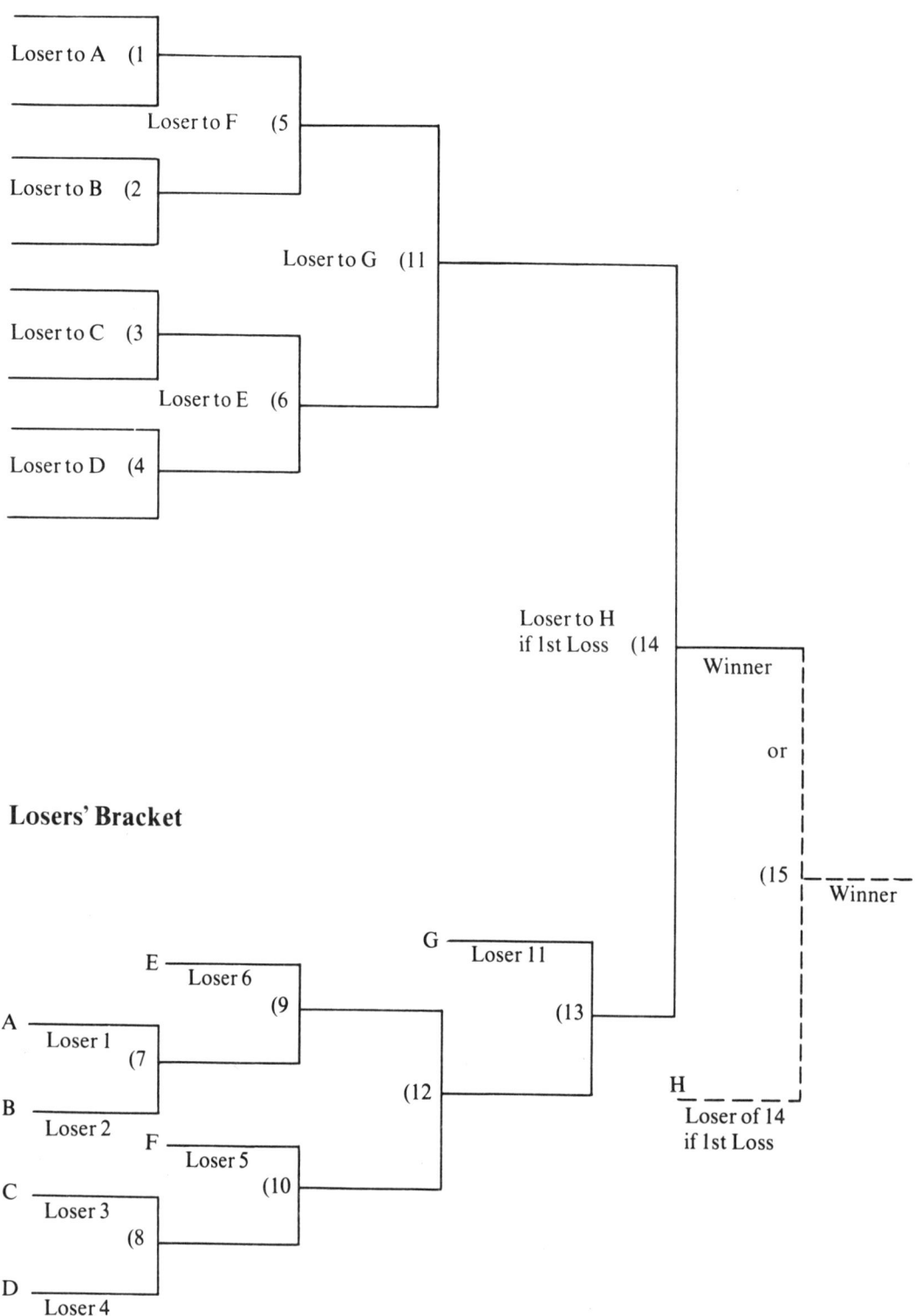

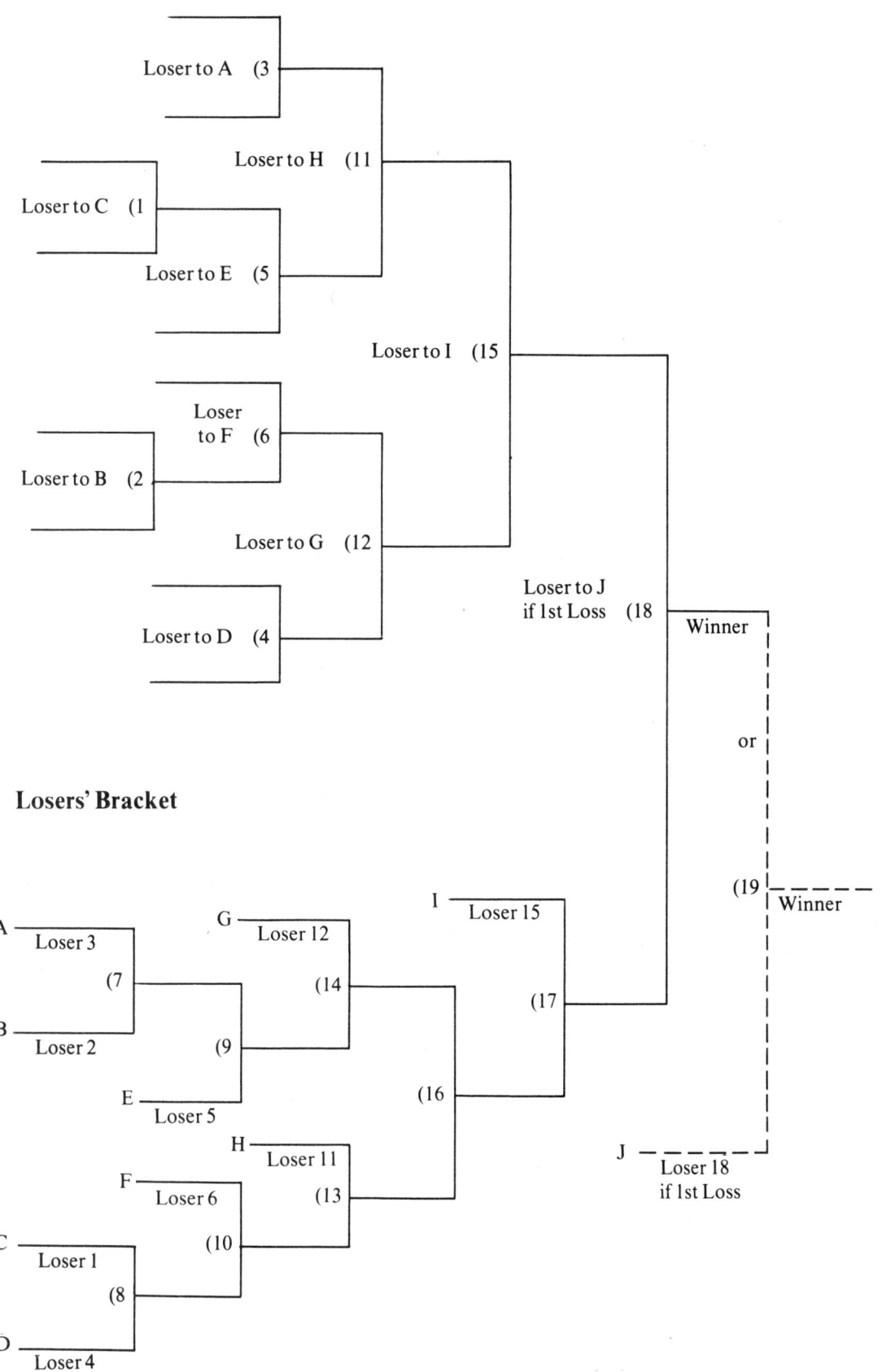

12 Teams

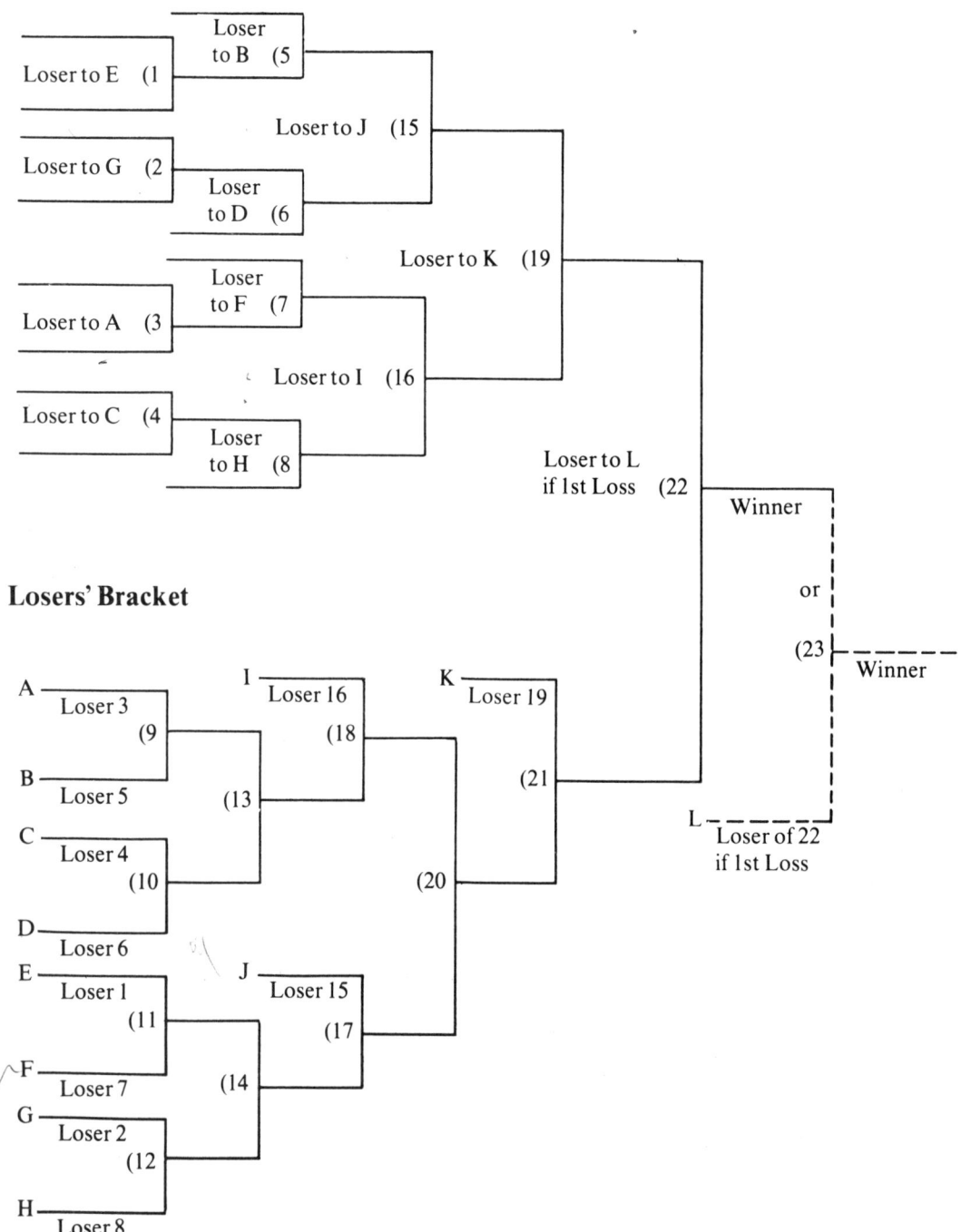

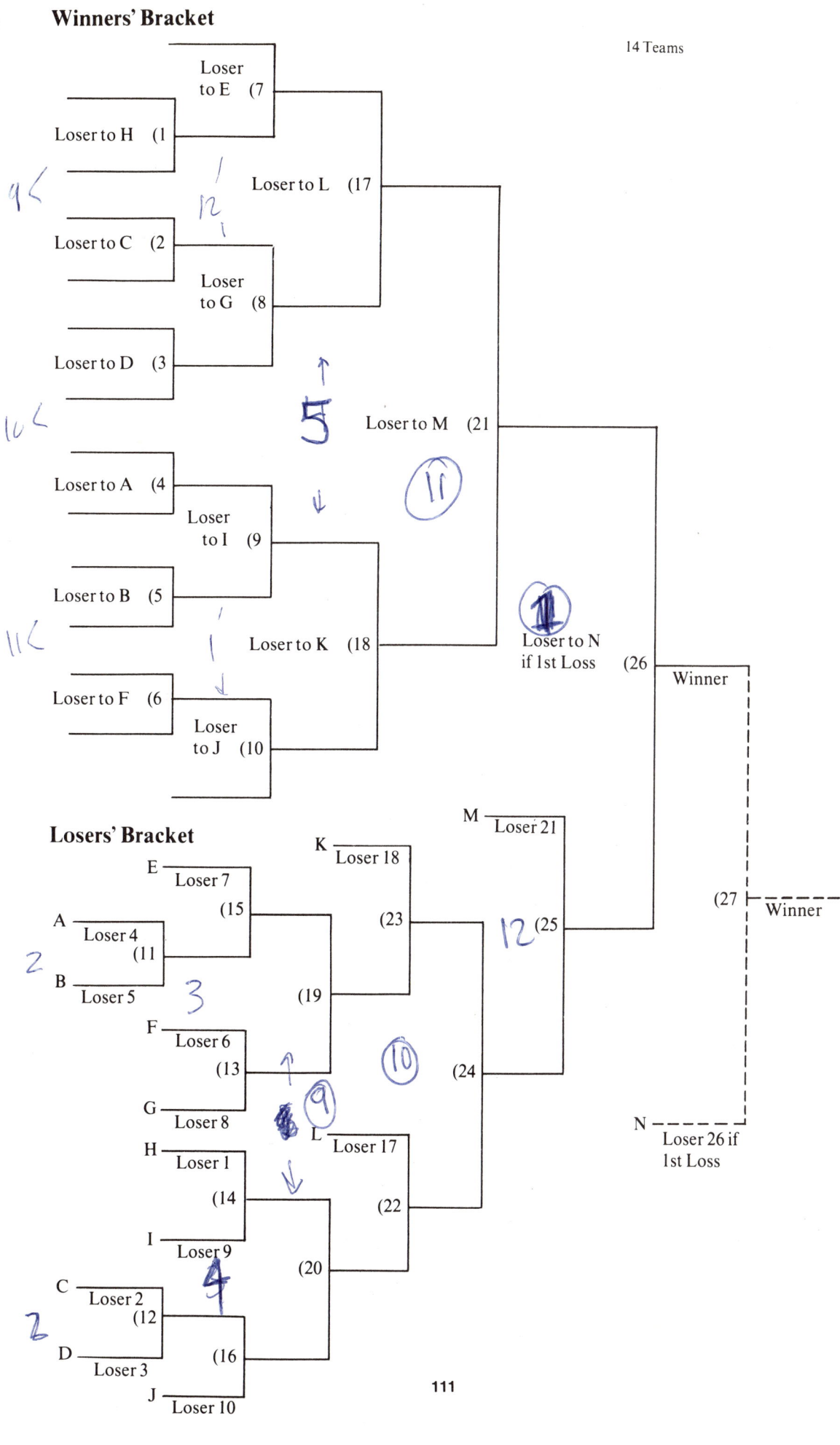

111

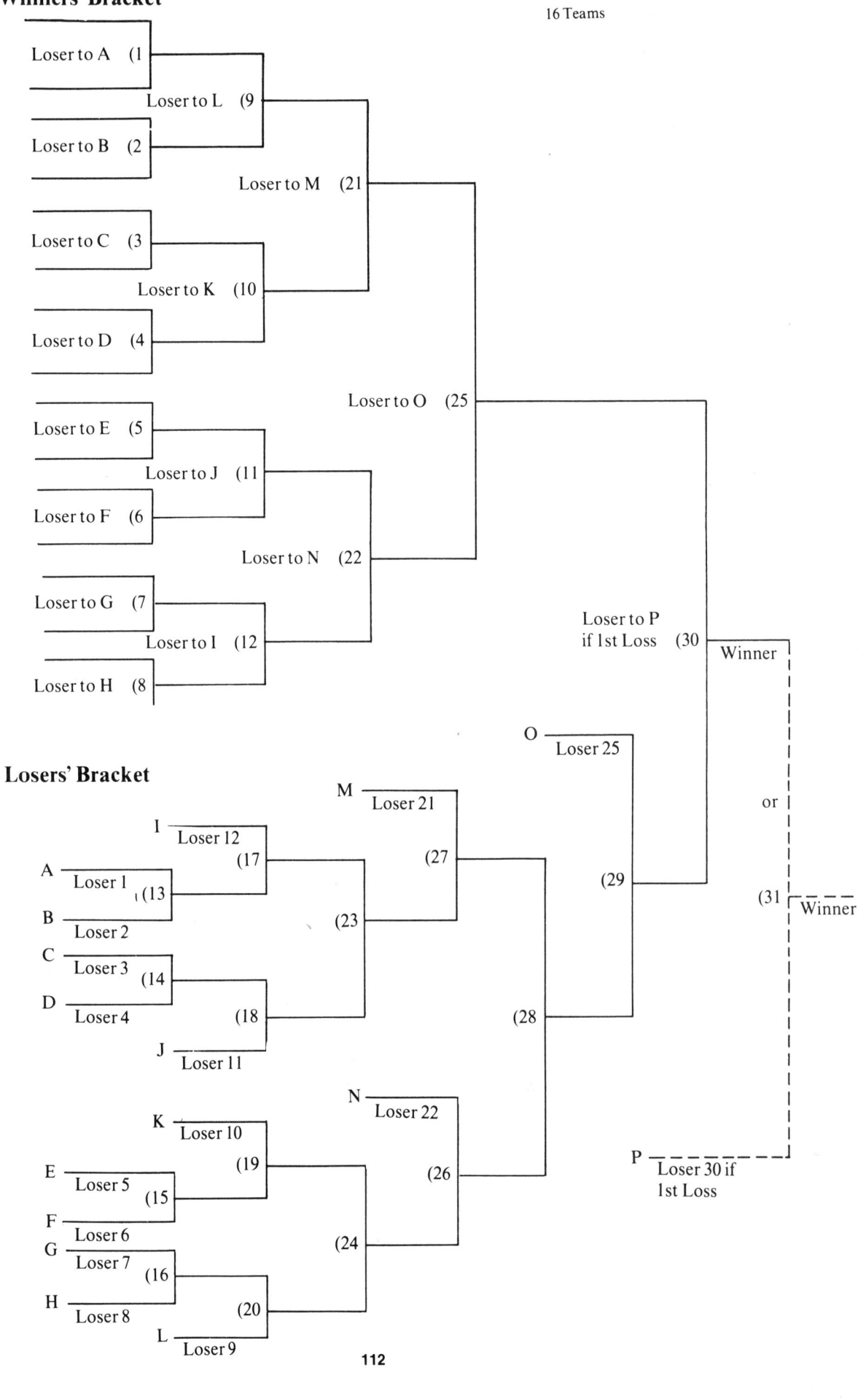

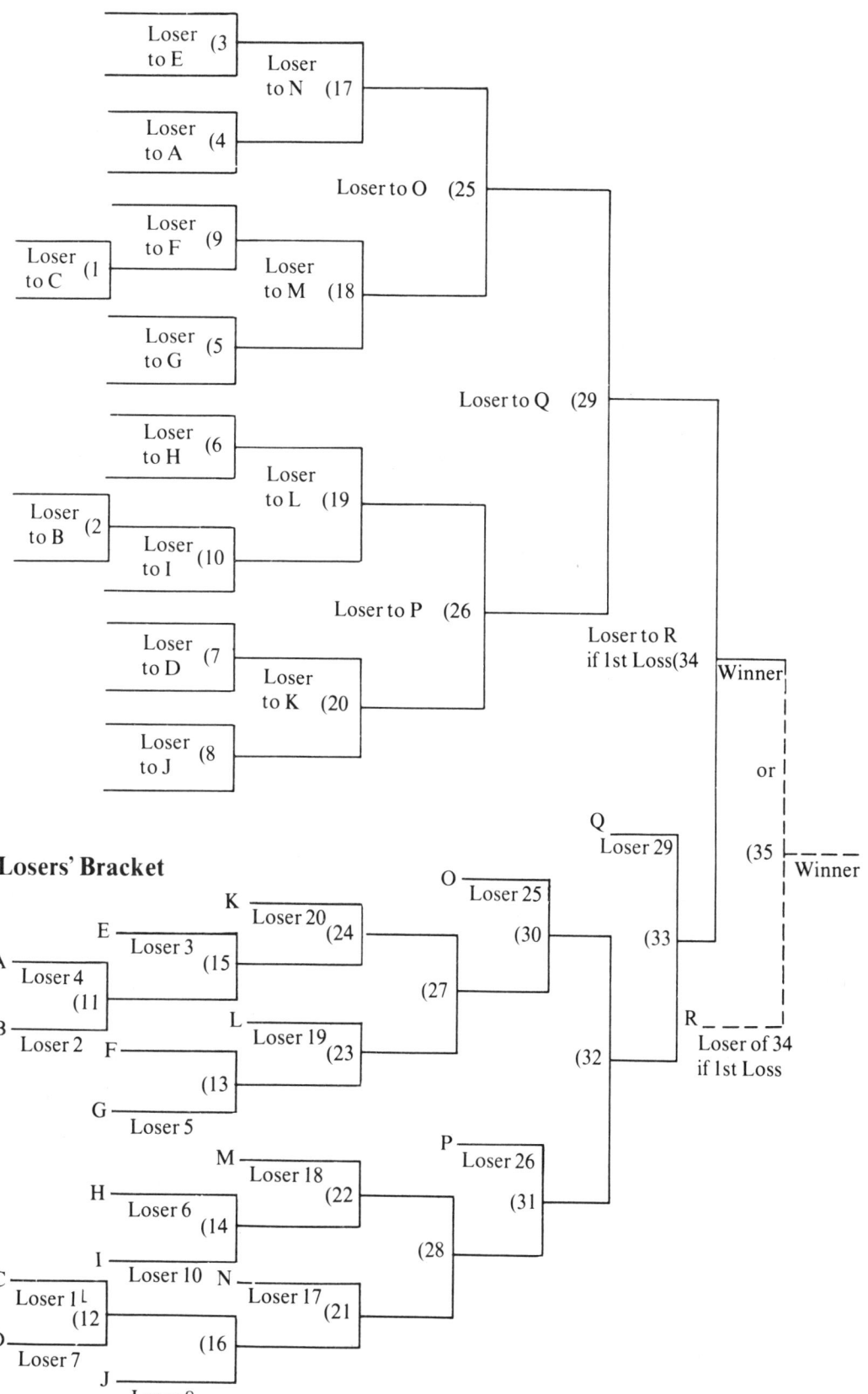

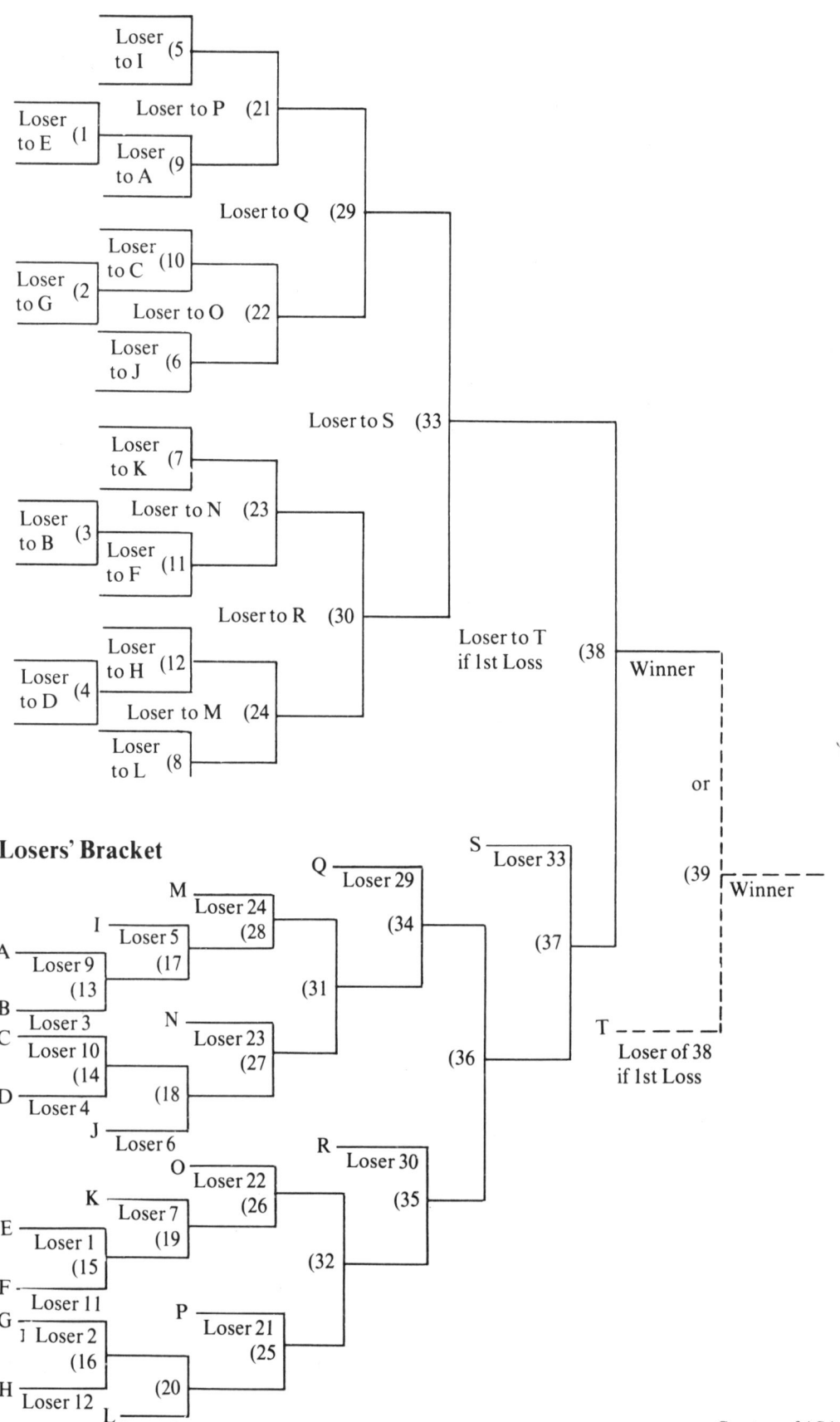

Courtesy of ASA

index

A

Accuracy, in throwing, 57
Alameda, Calif., xii
Altered bat, 4
Amateur Softball Association, vii, x
Arch, in pitching slow pitch, 34
Arizona, xii
Arkansas, xi
Attitude, 37-38
Aurora, Ill., vi, viii, ix, x, xi
Austin, Tex., ix, xi
Australia, ix, 7

B

Backhand stop, 69
Backing up bases, 20-23
Back-of-the-box hitter, 40
Backspin, 34
Bad habits in pitching, 10
Ball, xiv, 4
    sizes, vii, viii
"Ball", penalty, 10, 15
Bamboo bat, 4
Bases, 3. *See also* First base; Second base; Third base
    backing up, 20-23
    bunts, 60-62: bases loaded, 19-20; squeeze, 62-63
    calling, 18, 60, 61
    running, 95-96
    sliding, 96-100
    slow pitch, 63
    stealing. *See* Stealing
    throwing out runners, 18-20, 50-51
    trapping runners between, 58-59
Bat, vii, xiv, 3-4
    choosing, 88
Batter. *See* Hitter
Batter's box, 90
Batting average, raising, 92-93
Batting practice, 8
    slump, 93
Bench, 2
Blocking the plate, 48
Bloomington, Ill., viii
Bueno Park, Calif., xii
Bunt, 17-20, 60-62, 102, 103-104
    catcher, 49, 50, 52, 60, 61
    drag bunt, 17, 67, 76, 94-95
    first base, 18, 19, 60, 61, 62, 66, 67, 102, 104
    hitting, 93-94
    infield depth, 59, 60
    outfield, 82, 83-84
    pickoff play, 52
    second base, 18, 60-61, 62, 68-69, 72, 102, 104
    slow pitch, forbidden in, 23
    squeeze, 62-63
    third base, 18-19, 60-61, 62, 75: fake bunt and steal, 76, 102, 104; squeeze, 62-63
Burlington, N.C., xiii

C

California, ix, xi, xii, xiii
   Fresno, viii, xi, xii
Calisthenics, 38
Called strike, 33
Calling the base, 18, 60, 61
Canada, 7
   Toronto, Ont., xi, xii
   Windsor, Ont., viii
   world championship team, ix
Cap, 4
Catch, of pop fly
   catcher, 18
   infield, 57-58, 59
   outfield, 78, 79, 80, 81
Catcher, 45-52
   calling the base, 18, 60, 61
   equipment, 4
   pitcher and, 14-15: knuckle ball, 34
   throws from 49-50, 51, 52, 70-71: pickoff, 66
Cedar Rapids, Iowa, ix, xi
Center fielder, 79, 82-83
Champions, lists of, xi-xiii
Championship. *See* Tournament
Change of pace, 33
Change-up, 33
   curve, 33
   drop, 33
Charging a bunt, 17, 18-19
Chattanooga, Tenn., xiii
Checking the field, 84-85
Chicago, Ill., vii, viii, xi, xii
Children. *See* Youth
Choke grip, 86, 88
Cincinnati, Ohio, x, xi, xiii
Clearwater, Fla., viii-ix, xi, xii
Cleats, on shoes, 5
Cleveland, Ohio, viii, xi, xii, xiii
Closed stance, of hitter, 89
Clothing, 4-5
Coaching, 7-8
   hitter, 87, 93: bunt, 103-104; hitting where pitched, 91; third base, 90
   infielder, 56, 57: force-out, 70
   pitcher, 39: distance for youth, 13; fielding, 17, 20; tipping one's pitches, 42-43
   runner, 96, 97
   signals, importance of, 105
   winning, overemphasis on, 105
Coach's box, 2
Code, 70
   catcher's signals, 46
Color, of equipment, 4, 5
Columbus, Ohio, viii
Competition, degree of, 92-93
Concentration
   pitcher, 37
   hitter, 89
Connecticut, ix, xi, xii
Consolation tournament, 106
Cool, keeping, 37
Covington, Ky., xi, xiii
Crowding the plate, 39-40
"Crow hopping", 28
Curve, 27, 29, 31, 32-33
Cutoff depth, of infield, 59, 60
   slow pitch, 63

D

Dallas, Tex., xi
Delivery, legal, of ball, 10-11. *See also* Underhand delivery
   change-up, 33
   follow-through, 11, 26-27, 28, 33
   slingshot, 12, 24, 25-27
   slow pitch, 14: warm-up, 43
   warm-up, 36, 39, 43
   windmill, 12, 25, 27-28
Denver, N. C., xiii
Detroit, Mich., viii, ix, xi, xii, xiii
Diamond area, of field, 1, 2, 3
Dimensions, of field, 1-3
Double elimination contest, 106, 107
Double play 18, 19, 67, 68, 69-70, 72, 73, 103
   infield depth, 60: slow pitch, 63
   third base, 76
Double steal, 104-105
Drag bunt, 17, 67, 76, 94-95
Drill, warm-up, 84-85
Drop ball, 29-30
   batting practice for, 93
Dropped third strike, 49-50

E

Elk Grove, Calif., xiii
Equipment, xiv, 3-5
Exposed jewelry, forbidden, 4-5
Extra-base hit, 71-72, 76, 83, 84, 96
   slow pitch, 85

F

Faking, 58
   bunt, 60: steal and, 76, 102, 104
   pitch, forbidden, 11
   throw, 59
Fall-away slide, 97-99
Fastball, 28

Fast pitch
  catcher, 45-46: equipment, 4
  decline, ix-x, 7
  hitter, 86, 87-88: bunt, 93, 94, 103-104; hit and run, 105; hitting where pitched, 91, 92; stance, 89
  infield: depth, 59-60, 63; first base, 65-68; reaction time, 55; second base, 68-72; shortstop, 72-74; third base, 74-76
  national tournament, viii-ix: lists of champions, xi-xii
  outfield, 79, 81
  pitcher, 12: fielding, 17; lack, 7; "stuff," 28-29
  playing field, 1, 2
  return, x
Fence, 1, 2
  pre-game check, 84
Field, playing, 1-3, 84-85
Fielding
  infield, 54-77: catcher and, 49-50
  outfield, 78-85
  pitcher, 16-23
Figure-eight delivery, of pitch, 12
First base, 3, 5, 64-68
  bunt and, 18, 19, 60, 61, 62, 66, 67, 102, 104
  coach, 95-96
  slow pitch, 63, 65, 68
  throw to, 16, 64: catcher's, 49-50, 52
  trapping runner, 59
Flint, Mich., viii
Florida, xi, xii, xiii
  Clearwater, viii-ix, xi, xii
Fly ball, 22. *See also* Pop fly
Follow-through, in pitching, 11, 26-27, 28
  change-up curve, 33
Force-out, 70
Fort Lauderdale, Fla., xiii
Fort Wayne, Ind., viii, xi
Foul line, 1, 2
  guarding, 76
Fresno, Calif., viii, xi, xii
Front-of-the-box hitter, 40
Fundamentals, 8

G

Game preparation, 84-85
Glove, xiv, 5
  catcher, 46, 47, 50, 51
  infielder, 56
  outfielder, 80
  tipping one's pitches, 42
Grip
  hitting, 88: bunt, 94, 95; choke, 86, 88
  pitching, 29, 31, 32: tipping one's pitches, 42

safety grip, of bat, 3, 4
  throwing the ball, 82
Ground ball, 55-57, 69
  catcher, 49, 50
  outfield, 80-81
Grounds, 1-3

H

Hall of Fame, 25
Hammer Field, viii, xi
Hancock, George, vii
Hayward, Calif., xi
Head-first slide, 97, 100
Helmet, 5
Hialeah, Fla., xiii
"Hidden ball trick", 8
Hit and run, 102, 105
Hitter, 86-95, 100-101, 103-104, 105
  helmet, 5
left-hander, 49, 67, 72, 73, 76, 91
  weaknesses, 39-42: slow pitch, 43
Home plate, 1, 2, 3, 13-14
  backing up, by pitcher, 23
  bunt and, 19, 61, 62, 93-94
  plays at, 48-49
  sliding, 97
  slow pitch, 52, 63, 68
  stance, of hitter, 39-40, 88-89: bunt and, 93-94
  trapping runner, 59
Hook slide, 97-99

I

Illegal pitch, 9, 10, 15
  "crow hopping", 28
  too fast, in slow pitch, 14
Illinois, viii
  Aurora, vi, viii, ix, x, xi
  Chicago, vii, viii, xi, xii
Indiana, viii, xi, 39
Indianapolis, Ind., xi
Indoor Baseball, vii
Indoor-Outdoor, vii
Infield, 54-77. *See also* Bases
  catcher and, 49-50
Injury
  checking the field, 84
  effect on batting, 87
  exposed jewelry, 4-5
  sliding, 97
  warm-up-related, 38
In-shoot, 30-31
Inside pitch
  catcher and, 47-48

hitter's weakness, 39, 40: slow pitch, 43
  where to hit, 91, 92
Instructional programs, 7-8
Interference, 48, 49, 73
International Joint Rules Committee on Softball, vii, 4
International Softball Federation, ix
Iowa, viii, ix, xi
Iowa City, Iowa, viii

J

Jacksonville, Fla., xiii
Japan, ix
Jewelry, exposed, forbidden, 4-5
Jogging, 38
Jones Beach, N. Y., xiii

K

Kenosha, Wis., xi
Kentucky, xi, xiii
Knowing the hitter, 39-42
  slow pitch, 43
Knuckle ball, 33-34

L

Lakewood, Ohio, xiii
Laminated wood bat, 4
Layout, of field, 1-3
League scheduling, 106-113
Left fielder, 83-84
Left-hander, 45
  first base, 64, 65, 67
  hitter, 49, 67, 72, 73, 76, 91
    pitcher: curve, 32; fielding, 19; in-shoot, 30
Levittown, N. Y., xiii
Lights, checking, 84-85
Line drive, 79-80
Little League, 20
Little Rock, Ark., xi
Long grip, 88
Long Island, N. Y., xi
Losing sight, of ball, 80, 83
Louisiana, ix, xii
Louisville, Ky., xiii
Low rise, 31-32

M

Manager, 8
  hitter, 93: bunt, 103-104
  infield, 55, 56
  pitcher, 39
  winning, overemphasis on, 105

Manila, Philippines, ix
Mask, catcher's, 4
  pop fly, 48
Maumee, Ohio, xiii
Measurement, of field, 1-3
Medium grip, 88
Melbourne, Australia, ix
Metal bat, 3
Mexico City, Mexico
  world tournament, vi, ix
Miami, Fla., xi, xiii
Michigan, viii, xiii
  Detroit, viii, ix, xi, xii, xiii
  Midland, Dow Chemical, viii, ix, xi
Midland, Mich.
  Dow Chemical, viii, ix, xi
Milwaukee, Wis., viii, xiii
Minneapolis, Minn., xi
Minnesota, xi
Missouri, xi
Mitt, 5

N

National Fastball League, viii
National tournament, viii-ix, x, 25, 68
  list of champions, xi-xiii
Nebraska, xiii
New Orleans, La., ix, xii
Newport, Ky., xiii
New York, state, xi, xiii
"No pitch," 15
North Carolina, xiii

O

Obstacles, 1
  checking for, 84
Offensive strategy, 102-105
Ohio, viii, x, xi, xii, xiii
Oklahoma, ix, xi, xii
Oklahoma City, Okla., ix
Older persons, x
Omaha, Nebr., xiii
On-deck circle, 2, 89-90
Ontario, Canada, viii, xi, xii
Open stance, in hitting, 89
Opposite field hitter, 40
Orange, Calif., ix, xii
Oregon, viii, xi, xii
Orlando, Fla., xii
Out
  altered bat, 4
  bunting foul on third strike, 66
  double play. *See* Double play

tagging runner, 48-49, 66, 71
throwing runner out, 18-20, 50-51
Outfield, 78-85
Outfield relay, 71-72, 73-74
slow pitch, 74
Outside pitch
catcher and, 47
hitter's weakness, 39, 40, 41: slow pitch, 43
where to hit, 91, 92

P

Parma, Ohio, xiii
Pattern pitching, 42
Penalties
altered bat, 4
interference, 48, 49, 73
pitching, 10, 15, 28: too fast, in slow pitch, 14; warm-up violations, 12
Pennsylvania, xi, xiii
Philippines, ix
Phoenix, Ariz., xii
Physical defects, 87
Pickoff play, 51-52, 66
Pitch, regulation, 10-12
Pitcher, 36-43
fast-pitch decline and return, ix-x, 7
fielding, 6-23
rookie, 6-15, 16
style and "stuff", 24-34
Pitcher's plate, 1, 2, 13
Pittsburgh, Pa., xiii
Plastic bat, 4
Playing field, 1-3
pre-game check, 84-85
Pop fly, or pop-up
catcher, 48
infield, 57-58, 59
outfield, 78, 79, 80, 81
Portland, Oreg., viii, xi, xii
Positions
infield, 59-60: slow pitch, 63
outfield, 81-82
Practice session, 7-8, 16
getting out of slump, 93
Preparation, game, 84-85
Presentation position, 6, 10
tipping one's pitches, 42
warm-up, 43
Protective equipment, for catcher, 4
Pull hitter, 40
Pump motion, in windmill delivery, 28
tipping one's pitches, 42
Puerto Rico, ix
Putout, 79

Q

"Quick pitch", 8

R

Racine, Wis., viii
Reaction time, 55
Reading, Pa., xi
Regular depth, infield, 59, 60
slow pitch, 63
Regulation pitch, 10-12
Rhythm, breaking pitcher's, 89-90
Right fielder, 82
Rise ball, 26, 29, 31-32
hitter, 92, 93: bunt, 94; stance, 89; swing, 90; weakness, 41
Rise-curve, 33
Rochester, N. Y., xi
Rock Island, Ill., viii
Rohs, Elmer, 25
Rookie pitcher, 6-15, 16
Rotation, putting on ball, 11, 29, 30-32, 34
Round robin, 106
women's world championship, ix
Rubber, pitching, 8, 12-13, 14, 26, 38, 39
Rundowns, 58, 59
Runners, 95-99
helmet, 5
slow pitch, 100
tagging, 48-49, 66, 71
throwing out, on bunt, 18-20
trapping, 58-59

S

Sacramento, Calif., xi
Sacrifice bunt, 18, 72, 93-94, 103-104
Safety grip, of bat, 3, 4
Safety measures
catcher's equipment, 4
exposed jewelry forbidden, 4-5
helmet, 5
metal bat, 3
Salt Lake City, Utah, xii
San Antonio, Tex., xii
Santa Rosa, Calif., xi
Satellite Beach, Fla., xiii
Scheduling, 106-113
Scooping ball, in bunt, 17, 18
Screwball, 30-31
Seattle, Wash., xi
Second base, 3, 68-72
backing up, by pitcher, 20, 21, 22
bunt and, 18, 60-61, 62, 68-69, 72, 102, 104
catcher's throw to, 50, 51

extra-base hit, 96
hit and run, 102, 105
signals and, 46
slow pitch, 63, 72
trapping runner, 59
Self-confidence, 37-38
Sheboygan, Wis., xiii
Shirt, 4
Shoes, 5
Short-center fielder, 85
Shortstop, 72-74
    bunt, 60, 61-62: fake, 76, 102, 104; squeeze, 62-63
    double play, 70
    slow pitch, 63, 74
Signals, 70
    catcher's, 46: pickoff, 52
    coach, 105: first base, 96; third base, 90
Single-elimination contest, 106
Sliding, 96-100
Slingshot delivery, of pitch, 12, 24, 25-27
Slow pitch, x
    bunting forbidden, 23
    catcher, 52: equipment, 4
    hitter, 91, 100-101
    infield: first base, 63, 65, 68; outfield relays, 74; positions, 63; reaction time, 55; second base, 63, 72; shortstop, 63, 74; third base, 63, 77
    lists of champions, xiii
    outfield, 85
    pitching, 12, 14-15, 34, 43
    playing field, 1, 2
    runner, 100
Slump, batting, 93
Sole, of shoe, 5
South Bend, Ind., xi
Southgate, Mich., xiii
Speed, of pitch, 14
Spikes, on shoes, 5
Spin, putting, on ball, 29, 30, 31, 33-34
Spring, John, viii
Springfield, Mo., xi
Springfield, Ohio, xiii
Square stance, of hitter, 89
Squeeze, 62-63
Stalling, 8
Stance
    catcher, 46-47
    hitter, 39-40, 88-89: bunt, 93-94
    infield, 55, 56
    pitcher, 8, 9: follow-through, 28; slingshot delivery, 26; slow pitch, 14; windmill delivery, 27
Standing away from plate, 40
Stealing, 50-51, 70-71, 73, 96
    double steal, 104-105
    hit and run, 102, 105

    steal and bunt, 102, 104
    third base, 75-76: fake bunt and, 76, 102, 104
Sterkel, Harvey, x, 25
Straight-in slide, 97
Strategy
    offensive, 102-105
    pitching, 39: slow pitch, 43
Stratford, Conn., ix, xi, xii
Stride, of hitter, 90
    bunt, 95
Strikeout, ix
Strike
    called, 33
    hitter's weakness, 40
    slow pitch, 34
    third: dropped, 49-50; foul bunt, 66
Strike zone, 31, 33, 34, 40
"Stuff", putting, on ball, 11, 28-29
    change of pace, 33
    change-up, 33: curve, 33; drop, 33
    curve, 27, 29-31, 32-33
    distance of pitch, 13
    drop ball, 29-30, 93
    in-shoot, 30-31
    knuckle ball, 33-34
    rise ball. See Rise ball
    warm-up, 39
Style, pitching, 24-34
Sun, losing ball in, 80, 83
Sunnyvale, Calif., xi
Swing, of batter, 90, 91
    slow pitch, 100, 101

T

Tagging the runner, 49-49, 66, 71
Taking the throw, 64, 65-66, 70-71
Temperament, 37-38
Tennessee, xiii
Test, 8
Texas, ix, xi, xii
Third base, 3, 74-77
    backing up, by pitcher, 20, 21, 22, 23
    bunt and, 18-19, 60-61, 62, 75: fake, 76, 102, 104; squeeze, 62-63
    catcher's throw to, 50
    coach, 46, 90, 96, 97
    slow pitch, 63, 77
    trapping runner, 59
Throwing, 57. See also Pitcher
    grip, 82
    outfield, 81
    pitcher, 16
Throwing runner out, 18-20, 50-51
Throws, taking, 64, 65-66, 70-71
Tight infield depth, 63

Tipping one's moves
   pitches, 42-43
   signals, 46
Toledo, Ohio, xi, xiii
Toronto, Ont., Can., xi, xii
Tournament
   national, viii-ix, x, 25, 68: lists of champions, xi-xiii
   scheduling, 106-113
   warm-up: drill, 85; injury related to, 38
   world, vi, ix
Trapping runner, 58-59
Triple play, 18
Tucson, Ariz., xii
Tulsa, Okla., xi, xii

U

Umpire, 37, 66
   illegal pitch, 10: "crow hopping", 28; too fast, in slow pitch, 14
   interference, 48, 49
   strike call, 40
Underhand delivery, viii, ix, 10-11, 14, 25
   drop ball, 29-30
   slow pitch, 34
   warm-up, 39
Underhand toss, 62, 70
Undershirt, 4
Underswing, 90
Uniform, 4-5
Utah, xii

V

Virginia, xiii
Virginia Beach, Va., xiii

W

Walsh, Chick, viii
Warm-up drill, 84-85
Warm-up pitch, 12, 15, 36, 38-39
   slow pitch, 43
Washington, state, xi
Waukegan, Ill., viii
Weakness, hitter's, 39-42
   slow pitch, 43
Whittier, Calif., xii
Wild pitch, 47
Wild throw, 57, 61
Wind direction, 48
Windmill delivery, of pitch, 12, 25, 27-28
Windsor, Ont., Can., viii
Windup, 11-12, 14
   slingshot, 26
   tipping one's pitches, 42
   warm-up, 36, 39
   windmill, 27: pump, 28
Winning, overemphasis on, 105
Wisconsin, viii, xi, xiii
Women, 12
   playing field, 1, 2
   return of fast pitch, x
   tournament: national, viii, ix, x, xii-xiii; world, ix
Wooden bat, 4
Workout, 8
World tournament, vi, ix

Y

York, Pa., xiii
Youth, x, 7
   hitter, 87, 88, 90, 92-93
   infield, 57, 58
   pitcher, 11: distance, 13; fielding, 20; style, 25; "stuff," 28-29
   winning, overemphasis on, 105

Z

Zollner, Pistons, viii, xi, 25